HEALTH PSYCHOLOGY SERIES

Gloria R. Leon, Series Editor

THE

PEDIATRIC

PSYCHOLOGIST

ISSUES IN PROFESSIONAL DEVELOPMENT AND PRACTICE

LIZETTE PETERSON
CYNTHIA HARBECK

RESEARCH PRESS

2612 NORTH MATTIS AVENUE
CHAMPAIGN, ILLINOIS 61821

Advisory Editor, Frederick H. Kanfer

Cover design by Jack Davis

Composition by Circle Type Corp.

ISBN 0-87822-296-0

Library of Congress Catalog Card Number 88-61409

*To my constant companion
during the course of
this book: for Ged.*

L.P.

*To my parents:
for their love and encouragement.*

C.H.

Contents

Foreword

This book provides an important advance in the professional identification of the pediatric psychologist. In it, Peterson and Harbeck have done a superb job of discussing the professional issues most central to pediatric psychology and in describing the research and practice that characterize this exciting field.

One particular virtue of the book is its clear and concise examination of the field of pediatric psychology—its historical roots, current status, and challenges for the future. A further strength lies in its detailed descriptions of case management procedures. Such perspectives will be invaluable for education in many areas of psychology and medicine. In addition, psychologists, physicians, and other health professionals who work with children will learn a great deal that they can apply to their own work with pediatric patients.

In my view, a major contribution of this book is its developmental perspective. Peterson and Harbeck point to the importance of a strong knowledge of normal development in understanding a sick child's cognitions about illness, injury, and death. Too often, those treating or conducting case management outcome research with children fail to recognize how the child's interpretation of the situation will affect his or her response to medical and psychological procedures. One also needs to appreciate that the nature and complexity of beliefs about illness and hospital procedures will be subject to developmental changes. As the authors urge, courses in normal development are crucial for the adequate training of the pediatric psychologist or, for that matter, for anyone working with children and families.

This book appears at a time when there is a great deal of discussion within the field of psychology about the professional training of psychologists and the designation of new specialty areas. Some argue that health psychology and pediatric psychology should be identified and credentialed as particular specialty areas with distinct curricula and training opportunities. Others view health psychology and pediatric psychology as specializations within clinical psychology, with all students receiving a comprehensive grounding in clinical assessment and intervention procedures.

Specifically, the authors spell out a clear training progression, arguing that pediatric psychology's identification and general training model should lie within the domain of clinical child psychology. A specialization in pediatric psychology should then follow, gained through developmental and health psychology courses as well as through specialized practicum and internship experiences that build upon general child clinical training. A basic foundation in behavioral skills and family treatment procedures is also essential. Peterson and Harbeck recognize, however, that the pediatric psychologist has an identity different from that of the traditional child clinician and that he or she serves a unique role in medical settings and in settings tied to psychiatry units.

In addition to providing clear guidelines for professional training, Peterson and Harbeck emphasize the need for a strong research base in pediatric psychology, and they present an interesting array of ideas for further study. As they point out, the professional and scientific growth of pediatric psychology needs to rest on a critical evaluation of the efficacy of procedures used. The publication of these findings then provides a vehicle for disseminating this information to a range of health professionals.

The increasing numbers of clinically trained psychologists working in nonpsychiatric medical settings provide an excellent opportunity for psychology to continue its scientific and professional growth unencumbered by some of the "turf controversies" occurring in more traditional hospital settings. This book will be a significant influence in further delineating the role of the pediatric psychologist and in promoting professional growth in this important area.

Gloria R. Leon
University of Minnesota

Acknowledgments

The first drafts of this book were written while the senior author was on research leave from the University of Missouri-Columbia. They were scrawled in pencil on yellow legal pads and often composed as she wrote with one hand and held her newly arrived infant son with the other. This luxury was made possible by the extraordinary generosity of our fellow pediatric psychologists, who sent voluminous piles of reprints and preprints of their research, as well as sharing their scholarly impressions of the field. Special thanks go to Christine Davidson, Dennis Drotar, Charles Elliott, Sheila Eyberg, Susan Jay, Suzanne Johnson, Gerald Koocher, Annette LaGreca, Adam Matheny, Gary B. Mesibov, Donald Routh, Dennis Russo, Lawrence Siegel, Brian Stabler, June Tuma, James Varni, and Eugene Walker. We would particularly like to acknowledge the selfless contributions of Michael Roberts. Daniel Burbach's attention to early drafts of the book was also much appreciated. Finally, we owe a special debt of gratitude to Gloria Leon, who invited and commented on the text, and to Ann Wendel and Karen Steiner for their painstaking editing. We were grateful both for their confidence in us and for their constructive criticism.

We must also note, closer to home, that the final text was a direct product of the clever detective work of typist David Knipp, who always managed to discern what we really meant to say and often improved it a bit. The senior author appreciated the assistance and support of Carol and Amie Simpson and the patience of Andrew, Kestrel, and Geddes Homer. The second author similarly appreciated the encouragement and patience of several friends, including Addys Moreno, Vanessa Selby, and Alan Strathman. Any errors or omissions in this text remain the sole property of the authors, but for much of the positive qualities of the book, we are grateful to all of the above.

Introduction

Visualize the pediatric psychologist getting ready for work on a Monday morning. He or she may wear the traditional white lab coat of a physician, business attire, or more informal clothing for working prone on the carpet with a disturbed child. The psychologist may have obtained a background in developmental, health, or clinical child psychology prior to specializing in the assessment and treatment of physically ill or injured children. He or she may work in a large urban hospital, a suburban private practice office, a small town clinic, or a university psychology department.

While driving to work, the psychologist is thinking about the children to be served that day. The first child he or she will see is a 3-year-old boy scheduled for open heart surgery the next day. The psychologist's task is to prepare the child and family to cope effectively with this ordeal. The second child to be seen has headaches several times a week. The psychologist hopes that relaxation training and an incentive system will eliminate this child's headaches.

Thinking about the next child brings a worried frown. This diabetic 10-year-old girl persistently eats forbidden foods and "forgets" to check her urine for the level of free sugar. She faces complications such as blindness or even death if she does not learn to adhere to the diabetic regimen. Later in the day, the psychologist will work with an 8-year-old burn victim who is jeopardizing his health by defecating into the hydrotherapy tank, an action that temporarily ends the painful debridement of dead skin necessary to his recovery but that causes him to run the risk of infection. The psychologist hopes to give these children some tools to deal with the challenges that chronic disease or traumatic injury have imposed on them.

The rest of the day could be spent counseling a young mother of an infant who exhibits the symptoms of nonorganic failure to thrive, testing a mentally retarded heart patient in order to recommend school placement, working with the adjustment of a gravely ill leukemic child's family, and facilitating the physical therapy exercises of an arthritic child. In the course of an average day, the psychologist might also consult with nurses and physicians, do a presentation on childhood obesity for a group of nutritionists, and check on a current research project.

This job is rewarding but challenging; the position has been recognized for only a few years, and pediatric psychologists are still defining its parameters. In fact, the discipline of pediatric psychology as practiced today is less than 2 decades old, and the diversity of its contributions are just being realized. The field encompasses skills relevant to clinical, child, and health psychology but is identified as an independent discipline. The research base for pediatric psychology is developing rapidly, training programs are being debated and organized, and the number of employment opportunities is growing.

This book addresses the new and rapidly developing roles and challenges of the pediatric psychologist. The first part of the book defines and characterizes this new discipline. Next, a description of the field portrays its various roots in pediatric medicine, psychiatry, and clinical child psychology and suggests the need to return to ties in pediatrics and to build affiliation with developmental psychologists. Challenges unique to the pediatric psychologist are then considered, including aspects of the medical culture, the consultant relationship, and the developing child. The role of ill and injured children's general cognitive development—as well as their level of understanding of health, illness, and death—is examined, as are children's unique relationships to family, peers, and school systems.

After this discussion of the multiple challenges involved in the pediatric psychologist's role, the extensive and varied types of intervention that currently typify the field are explored. Perhaps the most important mission of this book is to describe for the reader the scope and depth of current practice in pediatric psychology. Such practice involves a range of interventions focusing not only on traditional psychological problems but also on psychosomatic illness, psychosocial problems such as child abuse, the management of chronic disease, and the diminishment of distress caused by medical interventions. We hope we have portrayed to the reader some of the excitement we feel about this field. The book concludes with an eye toward the future, with concern for a more solid research base, agreement on training needs, and increased emphasis on prevention rather than remediation.

Chapter One

Pediatric Psychology: Toward a Definition

There have been repeated attempts during the past 20 years to describe and define the professional identity of the pediatric psychologist. Early definitions emphasized the location of the service delivery: A pediatric psychologist was a psychologist who worked on a pediatric hospital ward (Wright, 1967). Now pediatric psychologists work not only on pediatric wards but also in specialized centers for chronic disease treatment, outpatient clinics, intensive care units, and dialysis units, as well as in private practice settings as consultants to physicians. Furthermore, they consult not only with pediatricians and medical staff but also with parents, school systems, state and county welfare departments, juvenile courts, and health and social service agencies (Roberts, 1986). Other early definitions focused on a broad job description. Wright (1967), for example, suggested that the pediatric psychologist is one who works to deliver psychological services of a nonpsychiatric nature to medically ill children. Others have included psychiatric or mental health interventions within the parameters of pediatric psychology (Johnson, 1979).

Some definitions of pediatric psychology have focused upon the background of the pediatric psychologist. Tuma (1975) suggested that pediatric psychology is a special branch of clinical child psychology and underlined the pediatric psychologist's need for broad clinical skills and an understanding of child psychopathology. Wright (1967) emphasized the importance of a sound background in basic developmental psychology, and Walker (1979) added the need for knowledge of both medical and behavioral psychology as prerequisites for the practice of pediatric psychology. Certainly, the credentials for working in the area have changed, as frequent employment of master's level psychologists has given way to demands for post-Ph.D. experience (Nathan, Lubin, Matarazzo, & Persely, 1979), and as minimal expectations of preinternship experience (Drotar, 1978; Tuma, 1980) have been augmented by the desire for ongoing practicum and predoctoral coursework in pediatric psychology (Ottinger & Roberts, 1980).

Finally, some authors have discussed pediatric psychology in terms of the tasks to be performed. This definition is the most complicated of all and, as will be seen later, involves tasks running the gamut within traditional psychology. These tasks include basic behavior modification of common childhood problems, treatment of psychopathy and psychosomatic illness, and interventions directed toward psychosocial problems. Pediatric psychology also involves the use of psychological techniques to deal with medically created difficulties, such as pain and anxiety implicit in invasive diagnostic procedures, and interventions to increase compliance with exercise or drug regimens in the treatment of chronic illness.

Lest it sound as though pediatric psychologists simply replicate the functions of other child psychologists in a different setting, it seems important to underline some of the differences that are implicit in the demands of the medical setting. Operating within an environment in which the disease model is utilized, the pediatric psychologist is frequently expected to quickly produce quantifiable or pragmatic answers to complex questions (Wright, 1979). Time is at a premium, and often children are admitted for only a few days, making lengthy assessment procedures and psychotherapy impossible (Roberts, Quevillon, & Wright, 1979). The pediatric psychologist, often not the primary care agent, must deliver services to the parent and child without disrupting the physician-patient relationship (Drotar, 1982). In addition to the physician, many other individuals must serve the child's needs and interact with the family, so the pediatric psychologist must function effectively in a multidisciplinary setting (Georgeopollous & Mann, 1979) and must be prepared to intervene at multiple levels and through multiple kinds of personnel (Drotar, 1982). Responsiveness to the special needs of medical staff and the unique stresses they encounter must also characterize the pediatric psychologist (Drotar, Benjamin, Chwast, Litt, & Vajner, 1982). (The pediatric psychologist's role in the medical setting is considered in more detail in chapter 2.)

Finally, the pediatric psychologist is paradoxically oriented toward preventing childhood social, cognitive, affective, and physical problems (Peterson & Ridley-Johnson, 1983; Roberts & Peterson, 1984a) in a system dedicated primarily toward remediation of the currently presenting physical problem alone. This difference in goals often requires the pediatric psychologist to work toward two goals simultaneously and to go beyond the medical setting to the community in order to reach children prior to the onset of a disorder (Walker, Miller, & Smith, 1985).

Pediatric psychology services are often officially tied to departments of psychiatry, although primary service obligations are to pediatrics (Drotar, 1982). Pediatric psychologists do not share a common job description with psychiatrists; for the most part, pediatric psychologists' skills are more behavioral, more research-based, and more concerned with measuring competency than with diagnosing and treating psychopathology (Walker et al., 1985; Wright, 1979). Thus pediatric psychology probably has more in common with behavioral pediatrics (Russo & Varni, 1982) than with psychiatry. In behavioral pediatrics, physicians apply psychological principles to children's behavioral problems. The two fields might be considered as reciprocal: The pediatric psychologist would treat serious psychological disturbances and might consult with or refer a child to a pediatrician if it appeared some physical problem were involved, whereas the behavioral pediatrician would treat major medical difficulties and minor behavioral problems and might consult with a psychologist if serious psychological problems were present (Walker et al., 1985). The recent establishment of such journals as the *Journal of Pediatric Psychology* and, more recently, the *Journal of Developmental and Behavioral Pediatrics* testifies to the continuing definition and extension of these fields of specialization and underlines the commitment of the fields to a solid research base as well as to clinical service delivery.

In order to understand this unique field—with its complex and sometimes counterintuitive constellation of responsibilities, therapeutic skills, and interdisciplinary allegiances—we must begin with a history of its development. In a way, the history of pediatric psychology may provide the best definition of the field.

HISTORY OF PEDIATRIC PSYCHOLOGY

Before Clinical Child Psychology—Early 1900s

The early 1900s predated the formal existence of pediatric psychology and indeed any psychological specialization devoted to the clinical prob-

lems of children (Gelfand & Peterson, 1985). Universities were beginning to acknowledge the importance of developmental psychology, but,
at the time, developmental psychology had a strong academic research
base, with little concern for applied problems in children.

In contrast, psychiatric and clinical psychological treatment for
children in the 1800s mimicked medical treatment, complete with
admission to a hospital, use of medication, and bed rest (Duffy, 1977). In
fact, the first clinical research in this country to focus on children was
conducted by medical students and psychology graduate students in the
early 1900s. For example, under the supervision of psychiatrist Benjamin
Rush, Charles Caldwell studied children's emotional reactions. Psychology graduate student Elizabeth Lord's Yale University dissertation on
pediatric central nervous system lesions was conducted under the direc-
tion of pediatrician-psychologist Arnold Gesell. Gesell's return to medical
school in 1912 to study pediatrics after receiving his Ph.D. in psychology
marks one of the earliest links between medicine and psychology.

In 1889, at the University of Pennsylvania, Lightner Witmer established the first psychological clinic and coined the term *clinical psychologist* (Achenbach, 1982). Although Witmer was on a pediatric journal
editorial board and often consulted with pediatricians (Routh, 1988), his
clinic primarily saw children referred by schools because of mental deficiency or academic difficulty. Similarly, in 1909, psychiatrist William
Healy began treating juvenile delinquents at the Juvenile Psychopathic
Institute in Chicago. Working closely with his wife, psychologist Augusta
Bronner, Healy later established the Judge Baker Guidance Center in
Boston. Experts in the history of psychology differ as to whether it is
Witmer or Healy who deserves credit for establishing the early roots of
clinical treatment for children (Peterson & Burbach, in press). However,
it seems clear that, although Witmer's system was closely affiliated with
schools and Healy's with the juvenile justice system, neither maintained
their strong early ties to medicine or developmental psychology. Instead,
the 1920s and 1930s saw the development of a relationship between
psychiatry and psychology that emphasized psychopathology in children
but excluded normal child development and the treatment of psychologically healthy children who were under special stress due to medical
conditions.

Emergence of Clinical Programs for Children and the Loss of Early Medical Ties—1920-1965

Ironically, as clinics for children spread rapidly through the country and
became accepted in both the academic and lay communities, clinical

child psychology's disaffiliation from medicine continued, partially as a result of the increasingly close relationship between child psychology and child psychiatry. At first, the schism between child psychology and pediatric medicine was promoted by a simple lack of interest. As Smuts (1986) has noted, "During the 1920s, when the new disciplines of child development and child psychiatry were being founded, pediatrics, itself a medical specialty only a few decades old, was too preoccupied with infant feeding and care of sick children to spare much time and energy for other considerations" (p. 7). A few years later, the problem was more serious: Child psychiatry was seen as an unwanted interloper in the field of pediatrics (see, for example, an article entitled "The Menace of Psychiatry" by pediatrician Dr. Joseph Brennemann, 1931). A strong prejudice against both child psychiatry and psychology developed within pediatrics; to some extent, this attitude has continued to the present time (Work, 1986).

This prejudice was most clearly apparent in the staffing of medical school faculty. Although the American Psychological Association (APA) suggested as early as 1911 that medical schools incorporate topics relevant to psychology into their curricula, only 7 of the 71 schools responding to a later survey included even a single course on psychology (Franz, 1913). Three decades later, fewer than a dozen medical schools had a psychologist on their faculty (Mensh, 1962). However, following World War II there was rapid growth in almost all areas of psychology, and medical psychology was no exception. In 1957, Matarazzo and Daniel published a survey conducted in 1955 revealing an average of over four psychologists on each medical school faculty. By 1960, this number had doubled (Nathan et al., 1979).

At the same time, the specialization of clinical child psychology had grown away from its roots in psychiatry to an area within its own right. It was increasingly characterized by a behavioral orientation and concern for normal development and competency building (Peterson & Burbach, in press). Thus the stage was set for development of a specialty in pediatric psychology.

Early Pediatric Psychology—1965-1975

Many individuals cite either Jerome Kagan's (1965) article entitled "The New Marriage: Pediatrics and Psychology" or Logan Wright's (1967) article "The Pediatric Psychologist: A Role Model" as the formal beginning of the field of pediatric psychology. Kagan focused on the advantages of early detection and prevention, arguing that certain classical developmental research techniques could pay big dividends in clinical practice.

He noted that a liaison between pediatrics and psychology forces the psychologist to confront real problems rather than theoretical research hypotheses, and he saw this situation as a growth-enhancing confrontation. Wright's article continued many of Kagan's themes, humorously suggesting that now that a marriage had taken place, we should soon experience a "blessed event," producing offspring of either "sex." One sex would be the psychological pediatrician (for which the current prototype is the behavioral pediatrician), and the other sex would be the pediatric psychologist.

Wright's (1967) classic description of the pediatric psychologist as one skilled in traditional cognitive assessment, behaviorism, and normal development and concerned with pragmatism and economy probably remains the best description of the role. Wright also foretold the need for a special interest group within a formal organization, and later that year a subcommittee of the APA composed of Wright, Salk, and Ross documented that over 300 individuals employed in pediatric psychology were in need of some formal representative body. The Society of Pediatric Psychology was formed the following year as a subsection of the APA's Division 12 (Clinical Psychology). The newsletter of this group began publication the next year and later developed into the *Journal of Pediatric Psychology*.

In the decade that followed, the field of pediatric psychology expanded at the most rapid rate ever. In 1964, around 11 psychologists were employed by each American medical school. By 1976, nearly 21 per school were employed (Nathan et al., 1979), and opportunities for psychologists in other medical settings were rapidly developing as well (e.g., Schroeder, 1979). The tasks allotted to psychologists in medical settings also broadened at this time. In comparison with psychologists in medical settings a decade earlier, these individuals were more involved in teaching, therapy supervision, and service delivery. The research base for pediatric psychology also grew and solidified. Methodological sophistication in combination with truly applied research questions came to be the criteria for research. (The research base for pediatric psychology will be discussed further in chapter 7.)

In other words, during the years from 1965 to 1975, pediatric psychologists were employed in a large variety of settings to perform an even larger variety of tasks. This diversity threatened to fragment efforts to establish a professional identity. However, the expanding organizational structure of the Society of Pediatric Psychology, as well as repeated efforts in the literature to describe the parameters of the profession, served to unify the field.

NECESSARY CROSS-DISCIPLINARY TIES

Now that unification within the field seems likely, it is important to turn attention toward establishing ties with professionals in other disciplines that have direct relevance to the practice of pediatric psychology. The most intimate ties to pediatric psychology, in terms of early training of most pediatric psychologists, are to *clinical child psychology*. However, the practice of pediatric psychology is conducted within the discipline of *pediatric medicine*. Finally, because the focus of pediatric psychology is upon children, the discipline of *developmental psychology* is relevant.

These three areas have traditionally been rather isolated, but, currently, there are trends toward cross-disciplinary collaboration between child clinical and developmental psychology, and between developmental psychology and pediatric medicine. Ironically, at present neither of these areas of active collaboration includes material central to pediatric psychology.

As the figure provided illustrates, general clinical child psychology is beginning to unite with developmental psychology in the area of developmental psychopathology (Gelfand & Peterson, 1985). However, this collaboration focuses solely on the most traditionally clinical aspects of clinical child psychology, such as the diagnosis of affective and behavioral disorders. The more applied aspects of clinical child psychology—especially those most relevant to the field of pediatric psychology, in which most patients typically are not psychiatricially disordered—have not yet united with developmental psychology.

Similarly, developmental psychology has a strong history of affiliation with pediatric medicine through joint membership of practitioners in both areas in the Society for Research in Child Development (SRCD) (Lipsitt, 1986). However, these ties have been between academic developmentalists and pediatricians who have strong interests in experimental child psychology. This overlap has not typically had clinical or applied overtones and most often has not involved topics relevant to pediatric psychology. As just one example, pediatric psychology was not even mentioned in a recent *SRCD Newsletter* (1986) that traced the history of the relationship between child development and pediatrics.

In other words, although the need for ties among these areas is strong, the necessary areas of collaboration differ markedly from those that already exist. The potential areas in which unification would be optimal for pediatric psychology thus remain within the unshaded areas of the figure.

A few examples of such three-way collaboration do exist. One concerns important work in pediatric psychology on hospitalized children's

Relationship between Clinical Child Psychology, Developmental Psychology, and Pediatric Medicine

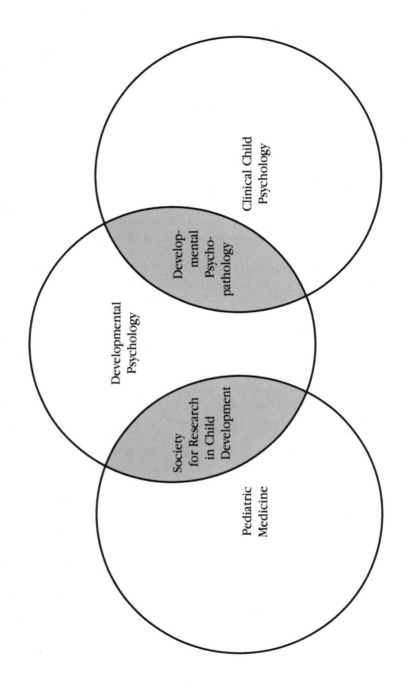

increasing cognitive understanding of illness at differing developmental levels (see review by Burbach & Peterson, 1986). The tradition of developmental psychology contributes a unique appreciation of children's cognitions, pediatric medicine offers unique information concerning the demand of differing illnesses and the needs for medication, and clinical child psychology provides the interviewing and intervention technology to use such information effectively. Developing three-way cross-disciplinary collaboration is one of the most important challenges for the future.

RELATIONSHIP TO OTHER FIELDS WITHIN PSYCHOLOGY

Finally, it seems important to consider ties to other areas within psychology. In our definition of pediatric psychology, we have tried to emphasize some of the aspects of the field that differ from traditional clinical child psychology. One important aspect is the medical setting. Within other branches of psychology, collaboration with medicine has already been established, and pediatric psychology has much in common with these subspecialties. Among the areas having the greatest commonality are *medical psychology* (concerning "the study of psychological factors related to any and all aspects of physical health, illness, and its treatment"; Asken, 1979, p. 67), *health psychology* (concerning the interface between health care professionals and psychology; Tuma, 1982a), approaches based on *psychosomatic theory* (concerning the relationship of biological, psychological, and social determinants of health and disease; Lipowski, 1977) and *biopsychosocial medicine* (concerning how biochemical, behavioral, and social contexts determine the process and outcome of disease and treatment; Varni, 1983).

In addition to the medical setting, pediatric psychology is distinguished by its need to focus on developmental issues in working with children. Here pediatric psychologists have more in common with behavioral pediatrics and with applied developmental psychology. Chapter 2 considers in more detail the impact of the medical setting and developmental concerns, and describes the unique demands the combination of these two factors places on the pediatric psychologist.

| Chapter
| Two

Unique Aspects of Pediatric Psychology

Although pediatric psychology shares a number of characteristics with other fields and subspecialties, two factors combine to distinguish it from other areas. The first factor concerns the nature of the professional's involvement in the medical setting; the second concerns attention toward developmental issues in working with children. This chapter will consider both factors. The role of the pediatric psychologist within the medical setting will be described first.

CONSULTATION/LIAISON IN MEDICAL SETTINGS

The demands of what has been termed the *hospital culture* (Drotar, 1982) can extend to any medical setting. These demands contain both important similarities to and differences from those of traditional academic psychology. Teaching, therapy supervision, research, and service delivery characterize pediatric psychology as well as academic psychology (Koocher, Sourkes, & Keane, 1979). However, one of the traditional rewards of a position in academic psychology is relative autonomy. In contrast, the pediatric psychologist is often dependent upon a hierarchy of other professionals for patient contact. At the top of this hierarchy are the physician-specialists, traditionally viewed as members of an elite group and accustomed to enjoying an attitude of authority (Tefft & Simeonsson, 1979) or even ownership regarding their child patients.

Physicians often have stereotypical notions of the role psychologists should play (Stabler & Murray, 1973), and the psychologist may have to weather a lengthy period of trial by fire (i.e., referrals of particularly "hateful" patients, impossible consultation requests, "lost causes," etc.) and negotiation with the physician to establish a truly collegial consulting and referral relationship (Drotar, 1983).

A major drawback to many physicians' understanding of the psychologist as consultant is not merely their tendency to regard the psychologist as subordinate, but rather their limiting of consultation requests to a narrow set of assessment questions. Such questions often include an emphasis on numerical quantification (e.g., an IQ test score) or on confirmation of the physician's own understanding of the case (Stabler, 1988). Physicians have a long history of using technical consultants to produce tightly quantified data—for example, that associated with serum levels or X-ray findings. This tactic fits well with physicians' reductionistic school-based training, which emphasizes building hypotheses by using empirical data to progressively eliminate possibilities (Roberts & Wright, 1982). However, this problem-solving strategy often leads physicians to ignore complicated and empirically nonsophisticated psychosocial information in favor of organic, disease-oriented data, even when the latter data are inappropriate to the question at hand (Conrad, 1975; Newberger & Bourne, 1978). The strategies used by the pediatric psychologist are likely to be seen as particularly foreign and inexplicable to such physicians.

Enhancing the Consultation Relationship

Several pediatric psychologists have made suggestions for establishing a sound physician referral relationship. Frequently mentioned techniques include accepting early, difficult referrals as given; using ongoing communication to sharpen and refine referral questions; demonstrating one's availability for consultation by attending regular medical rounds and by maintaining visibility in hallways and nursing stations; establishing credibility through both successful case management and research; and using strong personal lines of communication (Drotar, 1976, 1982; Koocher et al., 1979; Stabler, 1988). Demonstrating the utility of one's skills and the ability to adjust to medical norms (such as making brief, incisive case notes) also assists in forming a sound consultation relationship (Poznanski, 1979).

Recognizing obstacles to establishing good consultation communication is critical for the pediatric psychologist. Many such roadblocks stem from a misunderstanding of the role of the pediatric psychologist and the type of referrals that are appropriate. Other problems relate to "turf issues," or situations in which the pediatric psychologist is seen as usurping another health professional's role (Roberts & Wright, 1982). Turf issues can be problematic with any staff member but are particularly so with physicians, who as mentioned earlier often have a strong feeling of ownership about the patient, and with nursing staff, who are sometimes accustomed to being the sole direct care agents.

Stabler (1988) describes a series of issues that can present roadblocks to effective consultation with physicians, nurses, or other health care agents. First, lack of self-confidence on the part of the referral agent can result in a protective cognitive inflexibility that prevents psychological or developmental information from influencing case formulation; instead, the referral is made solely to validate the agent's preconceived notions. Similarly, poor self-confidence can cause the referral agent to avoid emotionally charged information entirely, resulting in an incomplete picture of the child's actual circumstances. Reassuring the referral agent that the request for assistance was a wise decision and involving the agent in history gathering to gradually blend in the psychological viewpoint are helpful in this situation. Demonstrating competence and confidence in assisting the referral agent will also aid in bolstering the agent's self-confidence.

Lack of information is the second roadblock to consultation listed by Stabler (1988). This problem is characterized by the referral agent's being unaware that consultation is indicated because of a lack of understanding of the problem area or the child's need within it. Education, whether through informal conversation or through more formal presentations such as clinical case conferences or seminars in developmental/behavioral pediatrics, can be an effective way of supplying the necessary information.

Lack of objectivity can also create problems in consultation, either through overinvolvement with the child, in which the referral agent may respond as if he or she had guardianship of the child, or through personal identification with the child, in which the referral agent's own experiences as a child or parent may interfere with conceptualization of the case. In such instances, the referral agent responds as an invested, enmeshed member of the child's ecosystem as opposed to an objective, caring professional. In dealing with such a situation, the pediatric psychologist must not only offer an effective solution but must also find a vehicle for making the referral agent aware of his potential lack of objectivity. At times, merely articulating a similar imbalance within others participating in the child's ongoing life or care may make the health professional aware of his or her own enmeshed role.

Finally, a lack of skill on the part of the referral agent can cause consultation difficulties if the agent's inability to manage the case threatens his or her professional dignity. In such a situation, the agent may label the child as a particularly difficult problem or the family as uncooperative or hostile in order to justify the inadequate treatment of the presenting difficulty. Stabler (1988) suggests a three-part solution to this problem. First, the pediatric psychologist must resist completely taking over the case from the referral source. "Swallowing up" the patient by assuming primary responsibility for the case (Roberts & Wright, 1982) will merely maintain the agent's lack of skill and sense of inadequacy. Second, the pediatric psychologist must attempt to reduce the sense of frustration in the referral agent. And third, the pediatric psychologist should evaluate the elements of the problem in close collaboration with the referral agent in a fashion that both avoids defensiveness on the part of the agent and teaches new skills.

All these methods of avoiding roadblocks to consultation pertain most closely to a consultation model in which the health care agent who has primary responsibility for the child makes a specific request for information or services from the pediatric psychologist. This arrangement is most often referred to as *direct consultation* (Schowalter, 1979). Other labels for the same relationship include the *noncollaborative approach* (Drotar, 1978), *coordination of multiservices* (Stabler, 1979), *psychologist as technician* (Salk, 1974), and *independent functions model* (Roberts & Wright, 1982). Several professionals have noted other methods of consultation that are being used with increasing regularity. Schowalter (1979) has described *indirect consultation*, in which the consultant attempts to improve the general emotional climate in the hospital by serving as a resource person for staff and patients who have concerns about such diverse subjects as policy formation, crisis intervention, and child development. Stabler (1979) has discussed three models, including the *direct consultation* or *resource model*; *process consultation*, in which physician and psychologist collaborate equally and treatment responsibilities are shared; and the *process-educative model*, in which the psychologist is a source of information and supervision for the physician's skill building. Roberts and Wright (1982) have outlined an *indirect psychological consultation model*, in which the psychologist has limited or no contact with the child but advises and supervises the physician or health care agent, as well as a *collaborative team model*, in which members of the health care team share case management. Roberts and Wright (1982) and Roberts (1986) have reviewed other conceptualizations of consultation as well and argued that no form of consultation is superior to others but that all can serve important functions for the pediatric psychologist.

In closing, we should not ignore the fact that many medical colleagues are open-minded, sophisticated in behavioral matters, and nondefensive in their requests for consultation. Such physicians receive inadequate attention in much of the literature on consultation and collaboration because they pose no problem. However, their existence and the enjoyment in working with such individuals deserve acknowledgment here.

Difficulties in Communication

Even after establishing a sound referral and consultation system, many challenges remain within the hospital culture. In most settings, the large number of extra patient demands as well as the large number of patients prevent any single discipline—be it medicine, nursing, or psychology—from meeting all psychosocial needs. In the medical setting, the psychologist does not have primary care of the child; in addition, he or she is also isolated from other psychologists and from community and educational facilities that otherwise might provide backup care (Drotar, 1977). The pediatric psychologist must therefore rely on the disciplines present in the medical setting. Unfortunately, these disciplines are organized in a deliberately isolated fashion. Varni (1983) refers to this arrangement as *multidisiciplinary* rather than *interdisciplinary* organization. Nurses do their rounds separately from physicians, who in turn meet only with other physicians, most often within rather than across specialty areas. Adjunct groups such as laboratory technicians, social workers, and clergy also have contact with the child, but fragmented interstaff communication is the norm rather than the exception (Naylor & Mattson, 1973). In addition, the pediatric psychologist's primary bond is most often to the house officer physicians, who are transient on the ward, typically being assigned to that particular rotation for periods of 2 to 4 months. The difficulties in maintaining good communication are clear (Bates, 1970).

Again, a variety of differing solutions have been posed by pediatric psychologists for dealing with these communication difficulties. Establishing clear lines of communication with key individuals such as the chief resident and head nurse proves helpful (Drotar, 1982), as does forming reciprocal communication functions with attending physicians (Stabler, 1988). Weekly conferences or ward problem-solving meetings have also been shown to help by presenting a regular, open forum for both case presentation and discussion of staff relationship problems

(Drotar, 1976; Koocher et al., 1979). Other official forums, such as pre-sentations to the interns' journal club or to the medical staff in grand rounds (Stabler, 1988) can form less regular but more far-reaching communications. Finally, these formal means must be steadily supple-mented by informal conversations (Geist, 1977), which the pediatric psychologist must engineer.

Obstacles in the Hospital Environment

We have focused thus far in this section on the people-based characteris-tics of the consultation/liaison setting. There are a variety of other aspects of hospital culture that also place unique professional demands on the pediatric psychologist. The aforementioned time pressures and need for rapid screening (Salk, 1970; Wright, 1979), the frequent need to combine crisis intervention with continuing care (Drotar, Benjamin, Chwast, Litt, & Vajner, 1982; Koocher & Sallan, 1982), the often heavy consultation demands that force pediatric psychologists to limit the scope of their work (Drotar, 1977), and the absence of physical space and privacy for therapeutic interventions (Drotar et al., 1982) all com-bine to create a unique, exciting, and yet stressful environment.

The hospital culture is only one aspect of the pediatric psychologist's unique role responsibilities, however. Other demands of the position evolve from the nature of the population being served. Those issues pertaining to serving a pediatric rather than an adult population are considered next.

DEVELOPMENTAL CONSIDERATIONS IN A PEDIATRIC POPULATION

The course of any illness or injury brings changes to which the patient must adjust. For children, these changes must occur on a nonstatic back-ground, for even the healthy child is involved in many different kinds of growth experiences. Because childhood is a time of establishing compe-tency in cognitive, social, and physical skills, it is especially important that the changes induced by medical intervention do not disrupt the normal developmental course of skill acquisition and developing self-esteem. Furthermore, because children's ability to understand, interpret, and cooperate with medical interventions is dependent upon their develop-mental level, psychological interventions must be geared to each particu-lar child's stage of development. It is therefore clear why one of Wright's (1967) prerequisites for the pediatric psychologist is a sound knowledge of child development.

This section will consider several aspects of child development that influence the practice of pediatric psychology. The developing child's general cognitive abilities; specific cognitive understandings of illness, health, and death; and misconceptions about medical interventions will be described. Psychosocial challenges at differing age levels will be discussed, and the effects of illness on these tasks will be considered. Finally, implications of the child's developmental level for assessment, treatment, and prevention will be outlined.

General Cognitive Abilities

Psychologists have utilized several conceptualizations for the study of children's cognitive abilities. Psychometric measurement of intelligence, stage theory, and information processing are three of the most disparate yet common methods. Such conceptualizations influence the way pediatric psychologists think about and study cognition, as well as yield methods of assessing any individual child's current level of functioning.

The Psychometric Approach

The psychometric approach to understanding cognition has been employed by clinical psychologists since World War II. This approach is the one best recognized by physicians, probably because of its focus on quantification. In fact, nearly half of referrals from physicians to pediatric psychology services involve requests for intellectual assessment (e.g., Drotar, 1977). Too often, physicians may have a misconception of the pediatric psychologist as only an intellectual assessor (Roberts & Wright, 1982).

The psychometric approach views cognitive abilities as discrete entities that can be sampled through written, orally presented, motor, or visual tasks. Certain knowledge and skills found to be representative of the majority of children of a given chronological age define "normal" intellectual ability. This approach attempts to place children on a static continuum in reference to same-age peers. This conceptualization is tied implicitly to its instrumentation—the intelligence test, which allows the child's cognitive abilities to be sampled and normatively evaluated. Intelligence tests are constructed to be highly reliable or consistent across measurement occasions and are judged by their predictive validity—how well they predict the child's ability to succeed in educational endeavors.

Infant intelligence tests, focusing on children less than 12 months old, are less reliable and valid than are tests for older children. The ability of such tests to predict later scholastic ability increases for tests designed for children ages 1 to 3 (Brucefors, 1972; Klackenberg-Larsson & Stensson, 1968), and the closer together in time successive tests are adminis-tered, the stronger the correlation between scores. The most commonly used tests of intelligence in young children are the Bayley Scales of Infant Development, the Denver Developmental Screening Test, and the Stan-ford-Binet (Lewis, 1976). The Stanford-Binet and the Wechsler Intelli-gence Scale for Children have been the most commonly employed tests for school-age children. The Kaufman Assessment Battery for Children is a relatively new but exciting instrument for intellectual assessment. Because it has special norms for non-English-speaking, hearing impaired, and learning disabled children, it is likely to be used increasingly by the pediatric psychologist.

Referral questions dealing with intellectual assessment may be prompted by a variety of concerns. We ourselves have been asked to perform intellectual assessments when the real questions ranged from "Why is this child noncompliant; can't she understand the importance of this regimen?" to "Why won't this child answer my medical history ques-tions?" to "This patient seems a little strange. I wonder why?" Thus it is particularly important to ascertain the reason for a request for intellec-tual assessment. Legitimate concerns involve issues such as school placement, presence of a learning disability in addition to a medical problem, or chemotherapy-induced intellectual deficits.

Considerable controversy surrounds the use of IQ tests, including charges that the tests are ethnically biased. Currently, the data suggest that IQ tests actually overestimate rather than underestimate the school performance of minority children (Cole, 1981). That is, IQ tests predict that minority children will perform better in school than they actually do, even though they also predict that minority children as a group will perform less well than other children. Why this discrepancy? Some experts suggest it occurs because the cultural and linguistic bias in IQ tests is simply a reflection of the even greater bias inherent in the school system. Despite concerns about bias in IQ tests, there is some evidence that recommendations for special placement derived from IQ tests are less ethnically biased than are recommendations from other sources, such as school teachers and counselors (Reschly, 1981). Thus, although tests of perceptual and mental ability must always be interpreted within the child's linguistic, cultural, and socioeconomic background, they do have some real value. In addition, there are some developing tools, such as the System of Multicultural Pluralistic Assessment (SOMPA), that can assist the testgiver in integrating test scores with demographic factors. This method considers such variables as urban acculturation and family structure, size, and income (Mercer, 1973, 1979). Some recently devel-oped tests (e.g., the Kaufman Assessment Battery for Children) contain special minority norms as well. (For further discussion of these issues, see Reschly, 1981; Scarr, 1981.)

Finally, awareness of alternate tests of ability is also important. Psychology long ago abandoned the concept of a culture-free test, but some instruments do appear to have less cultural bias than traditional intellectual assessment instruments. The Leiter International Performance Scale, for instance, uses sequences of colors to assess nonverbal reasoning, and Raven's Progressive Matrices use only a series of unusual visual cues to assess the child's ability to perform analytic thinking. Uzgiris and Hunt (1975) have evolved assessment techniques that employ Piagetian developmental concepts, which may be less culturally biased than other approaches. (See the following section for further discussion of the implementation of Piaget's developmental theory.) Drawing tasks such as the Bender Gestalt can also examine basic processes such as visual perception and hand-eye coordination. Tests of motor maturity such as the Bruininks-Oseretsky Motor Proficiency tests and tests of social maturity such as the Vineland Social Maturity Scale may also prove helpful. In all cases, focusing on the child's unique strengths and weaknesses as they relate to the current home and school environment is critical to unbiased testing. In addition, the child's motivation and proclivity to learn should always be carefully considered.

Stage Theory Approach

Stage theory is the second method commonly used to investigate children's cognitive abilities. Although some professionals have suggested using instruments based on stage theory to test basic intellectual abilities (e.g., Uzgiris & Hunt, 1975), stage theory approaches cognition in a very different fashion than does psychometric theory. Stage theory has viewed cognition in an idiographic rather than nomothetic fashion, placing the individual child not on a comparative continuum with other children of the same chronological age, as intellectual assessment does, but rather on the child's own continuum of developmental stages.

Piaget's (1970) theory is the best known and most frequently applied stage theory of cognitive development. Piaget described a genetically transmitted continuum of stages that he believed spontaneously unfolded as a child encountered the world through physical and social experience. These stages, Piaget asserted, were experienced by all children at their own rates. Furthermore, the rate at which children progressed through the stages was not even or steady; it was normal rather than pathological to have periods of little change interspersed with periods of rapid growth (Piaget, 1950).

Piaget described four major stages of development. During the earliest, the *sensorimotor period*, infants acquire the first primitive understanding of cause and effect and of objects in the environment. They establish mental representation, the understanding that objects continue to exist out of their own sight. They also develop strategies for seeking out desired stimuli. During the *preoperational period*, preschool children begin to use their expanding memory and mental representation to plan and to fantasize. A beginning ability to categorize events and to think logically is formed. Prior to the *concrete operational* period, school-age children have developed conservation ability, or the understanding that changing the container in which a liquid is held or the shape of a solid material (e.g., clay) does not alter the basic amount or properties of these substances. This understanding allows these children to think in a more mature and well-integrated fashion. During this time, ability to reason improves dramatically, as does the memory system, which becomes much more like an adult's. Finally, in the highest stage, the *formal operational period*, adolescents demonstrate the ability to consider several aspects of a problem simultaneously and to think abstractly in effecting a solution.

Achenbach (1982) noted that the competencies evolved within each stage bring with them a series of difficulties as well. For example, the fantasies of the preoperational period can produce frightening images of monsters and witches. The improved logic of the concrete operational period allows children to discover parental fallibility and may result in increased arguments and criticism of authority, whereas the adolescent's abstract logic may result in questioning the whole system of societal values. It is clear that understanding the basic cognitive errors committed by children in each of these periods—the gaps in children's ability to understand and interpret events as well as the strengths and skills they possess—is essential to the pediatric psychologist. Such understanding will not only make children's behavior more interpretable, it will also make communicating with children more effective.

Information-processing Approach
Information-processing theory has been utilized most often by experimental psychologists and developmental psychologists. Although this approach has a great deal of promise, few applications of information-processing concepts have been employed by pediatric psychologists.

Basically, the information-processing approach views the developing child as an active cognitive manipulator of the world. It focuses on the symbols the child creates to encode (i.e., describe and store) his or her understanding of stimulus events (Rathus, 1988). This conceptualization can be especially useful for examining cognition in very young children because information-processing assessment methods often rely on the child's nonverbal reaction to a stimulus rather than on a linguistically based response. It is thus possible to gauge a child's understanding of an object or a stimulus event before the child has the ability to verbalize this understanding. For example, infant memory processes can be tested by using a habituation-dishabituation paradigm. After a baby has been shown a picture or pattern and has habituated to it (stopped attending), a new but similar pattern is shown. At one stage, the infant may continue to show habituation, but at a later stage the infant will dishabituate and look more intently again. This finding demonstrates that the more mature infant has now stored an accurate picture of the first object in visual memory, can compare it to the second object, and can perceive the difference. Such comparisons allow us to track learning in a child as a cumulative process across time, beginning early in life.

Information-processing models could have a variety of both research and clinical applications in pediatric psychology. Treatment outcome research focused on interventions for infants with low birth weight could profitably use an information-processing paradigm. Small and relatively subtle increments in processes such as perception and memory could be tracked by using such techniques. Similarly, some researchers have suggested information processing as a method of evaluating handicapped infants (Kearsley, 1981) or of understanding how children first organize concepts by using language (Collins & Quillian, 1972). These techniques could also be used clinically to evaluate what a child remembers of past medical procedures or to evaluate the number of differing "bits" of information that can be successfully included in the treatment explanation offered to a particular child. However, unlike psychometric and (to a lesser extent) stage theory approaches, which have established clinical applications, techniques of information processing have yet to be adapted for clinical use and thus remain a matter for future intervention and research.

Researchers are just beginning to explore children's cognitive abilities relative to their beliefs about illness and health. Most of this research has utilized a stage theory orientation similar to that of Piaget, rather than information-processing or psychometric approaches. The next section describes some of this work.

Cognitive Abilities Specific to Illness and Health

Perhaps the best known developmental model of children's causal conceptualizations of illness was offered by Bibace and Walsh (1980). They questioned 72 children ages 4 through 12 about their understanding of the etiology of illness and identified six stages that roughly parallel Piaget's four stages. The first stage is labeled *phenomenism* because children in this stage conceive of the causes of illness as concrete and temporally or spatially remote phenomena. An example of such erroneous logic is seen in the statement "People get colds from the sun." This notion of cause and effect is similar to some of the logical errors seen in the late sensorimotor and early preoperational phases of Piaget's conception of cognitive development.

The second stage is labeled *contagion* because it is characterized by the identification of a person or an object as the source of the illness, as in the statement, "People get colds from the swimming pool." This type of "magical thinking," similar to preoperational thought, attributes the illness to the mere existence of the contagious object or individual and does not link the illness and the recipient through direct contact.

The third stage is labeled *contamination*, and within it children identify some object or action that is physically harmful as being the cause of illness. A typical statement within this stage might be "People get colds when they go outside without a hat." Such thoughts are characteristic of Piaget's concrete operational period.

The fourth stage is designated as *internalization* because, although children at this stage still concretely consider the ultimate cause of illness to be an external stimulus, they now focus on the internal effect of the stimulus—for example, "People get colds by breathing in bacteria." Swallowing is another concrete way in which the external stimulus might be seen to have its internal effect.

Stage five, the *physiologic* stage, is exemplified by the belief that specific internal physiological structures contribute to the action of the external agent—"People get colds from viruses that multiply inside the body," for example. This stage is viewed as parallel to formal operational thought.

The last stage is labeled *psychophysiological* to designate the belief that cognitions and emotions influence the internal processes of disease. Statements such as "People get heart attacks from being nervewracked" characterize this stage, which also parallels Piaget's conception of formal operational thought.

A small body of literature has examined both healthy and ill children's concepts of illness in a developmental fashion. Burbach and Peterson (1986) reviewed this literature in detail. Briefly, two types of studies have approached the problem. One type utilizes chronological age as a correlate of beliefs. This method is problematic because children of a given age may have very different levels of cognitive maturity. As discussed earlier, Piagetian theory suggests that development is neither linear nor age-specific. A second type of study relates developmental level, typically measured by Piagetian tasks, to beliefs about illness.

These two types of studies have produced a variety of often contradictory findings concerning the effects of cognitive maturity and health status. Burbach and Peterson (1986) described three major conclusions. First, a relationship exists between maturity and illness concepts. Young children who have yet to master the idea of conservation conceive of illness in global, nonspecific ways, without considering the psychological, affective, and social aspects of illness. They tend to confuse illness symptoms with the causes of illness and rely more on external symptoms than on internal cues. They often conceive of illness in a moralistic way—for example, as punishment for misdeeds—and feel little control over whether they become ill or not. Older, more cognitively mature children consider illness in more specific terms. They consider the psychological, emotional, and social issues pertaining to illness. They separate etiological agents such as germs and infection from symptoms such as fever and do not regard illness in a self-blaming fashion. They have an enhanced sense of control over illness and recovery.

Second, gender has no clearcut influence. In some cases, older boys tend to acknowledge illness and pain less than do older girls or younger children of both sexes, but even this difference is not always present or marked.

Third, the impact of prior illness or injury on illness concepts is unclear. Some studies (e.g., P. Williams, 1978a, 1978b) suggest that hospitalized children have more cognitively advanced concepts of illness than do healthy children. Other studies (e.g., Brewster, 1982) show no differences. Still others (e.g., Cook, 1975) argue that hospitalized children have less mature illness concepts. Differences in measurement technique as well as failure to control for variables like IQ may explain these findings. It could be argued that experiences with illness would result in more mature thinking about illness if one were well prepared and informed. In contrast, if the illness were stressful, it could be expected to retard all aspects of cognitive development, including thinking about illness. In any case, it is obvious that any explanations pediatric psychologists offer to children concerning illness must take into consideration each child's developmental level.

Far less research has been focused on children's health-relevant beliefs. Natapoff (1978) examined children's understanding of the word *health*, their beliefs about what constitutes health, and their understanding of health as a relative concept (e.g., "Can you be part healthy and part not healthy at the same time?"). He found that first-grade children described being healthy as performing certain behaviors, such as eating vegetables, and that they believed the outcome of being healthy was the ability to perform certain other behaviors, such as playing outdoors. Health was an absolute; one was either sick or healthy. Fourth-grade children were more inclined to describe general states, such as being in good physical condition, as "healthy" and saw the outcome of health as the ability to perform strenuous activities. They no longer viewed health as an absolute; one could be healthy in one respect but not in another. Finally, seventh graders had more complex conceptualizations of health, including aspects such as mental health. They perceived health as the typical state within which interactions of body, mind, and environment took place; sickness was perceived as a disruption of this typical state.

The literature on adults' health beliefs has been dominated by Rosenstock's (1974) Health Belief Model. This model suggests that health behaviors such as compliance with medical regimens can be predicted from individuals' beliefs about their susceptibility to illness, the consequences of illness, and the costs and benefits of intervention. Few researchers have attempted to apply this model to children. There is some evidence that, in comparison to older children, younger children have highly variable health beliefs, with more sense of susceptibility to illness and more frequent beliefs that the consequences of illness are serious (e.g., Dielman, Leech, Becker, Rosenstock, & Horvath, 1980). Some pediatric psychologists argue that such reasoning implies that young children are more amenable to modification of health beliefs than are older children (Varni, 1983).

Knowledge of health-relevant beliefs can thus be used to plan optimal health-enhancing interventions for children, as well as for improving communication with ill children. For example, the time at which young children have the strongest belief that they are susceptible to dental decay may be the best time to begin teaching dental hygiene, and beliefs in the seriousness of heart disease can provide an early link to sound nutrition and exercise habits. Likewise, awareness of pediatric patients' ability to interpret what is being said and to remember the essential parts of a message is critical for teaching children with phenylketonuria (PKU) to remain on their diets even in their parents' absence, for preparing children with asthma to self-medicate, and for convincing children with diabetes that they must save urine for testing. Preparing children for any medical procedures also demands developmentally appropriate communication.

Encounters with illness and injury may actually serve to expand a child's horizons. In his presidential address to the Society for Research in Child Development, Parmelee (1986) argued that minor childhood illnesses such as colds and gastrointestinal upsets provide opportunities for children to increase their understanding of self and significant others. Parmelee acknowledged that children's specific cognitive understanding of illness was important. However, he went on to suggest that the influence of children's illness could have a broader impact. He argued that children's general psychosocial awareness may be increased as children see themselves contract and then recover from minor illnesses and as they view parents and siblings undergo the same process. Although there has been no research conducted in this area, such concepts are richly deserving of research by both developmentalists and pediatric psychologists.

Like beliefs about illness and health, children's understandings about death appear to be developmentally specific (e.g., Hostler, 1978; Koocher, 1973), as will be seen in the next section.

Beliefs about Death

Spinetta et al. (1982) outline a developmental progression of well children's understanding of death. Children less than 2 years of age do not seem to comprehend the concept of dying, although they are extremely sensitive to thoughts of separation from loved ones. This lack of awareness is similar to other processes described in the sensorimotor period. Three-year-olds also do not fully comprehend the idea, but between ages 3 and 5 most children begin to be aware that animals, plants, and other people occasionally die. They are not yet aware that death is more than sleep and do not conceive of death as a permanent state. They also do not believe in the possibility of their own mortality. By age 6 or 7, paralleling the development of conservation skills, most children are able to approach the concept of death as final and as universal, and to understand that loved ones and even they themselves will die someday. This possibility is perceived as being in the far distant future, however. Even at age 8 or 9, children still do not appear to have a well-articulated understanding of the inevitability and finality of death. Such an understanding is made possible by the increasing logic and experience of the preadolescent, as in the processes outlined in the formal operational stage of development.

There is some evidence that the development of an understanding of death is accelerated when the child experiences a life-threatening illness (Bluebond-Langer, 1974, 1977; Spinetta, 1974). Even when parents and medical staff members do not openly discuss the possibility of death, children of elementary school age often demonstrate an awareness of their own mortality, with resultant fears of abandonment and separation (Spinetta et al., 1982). Obviously, this underresearched area is important for the pediatric psychologist who must work with seriously ill children of differing developmental levels and with differing concepts of health, illness, and death.

Recognizing the extent to which children accurately conceive of health and illness concepts and being aware of possible misconceptions are essential to communicating medically related information to children. Fortunately, the research base on children's cognitions and misconceptions concerning illness is growing rapidly. For example, as will be seen in the next section, the developmentally informed pediatric psychologist avoids describing anesthesia induction in terms like "being put to sleep," which can connote the same untimely end experienced by the elderly family dog, and likewise hastens to assure the young child that he or she need not worry about awakening prematurely in the middle of surgery.

Developmentally Based Misconceptions of Illness

Piaget (1970) outlined several cognitive errors made by children in the sensorimotor and preoperational periods that are characteristically resolved prior to the concrete operational period. Two errors relevant for the pediatric psychologist are the *naturalistic view of misfortune* and the concept of *intentionality*. In the naturalistic view of misfortune common to younger but not older children, bad deeds are automatically and inevitably followed by environmentally based punishment. This way of viewing the world explains the often reported belief that one's injury or illness is a form of punishment for misbehavior (Korsch, 1961; Sheridan, 1975). Children who view illness as punishment often have a superficially logical explanation for how their physical condition came about, as is seen in diabetic children who believe their disease is a product of eating too much sugar or in pediatric cardiac patients who believe that playing too hard brought on their ailment (Willis, Elliott, & Jay, 1982). A child who views illness as punishment may be reluctant to report symptoms of illness, and this reticence can dangerously delay medical intervention. Such a child also adds to the stress of illness the stress of guilt and anxiety over punishment.

The second Piagetian concept, intentionality, is not understood by preoperational children. Because they are unable to consider intentions when judging the outcome of an act, such children can often harbor misconceptions regarding the course of their injury or illness. Thus to explain to a 2-year-old that Daddy did not mean to scald her with hot coffee is meaningless; only the outcome is clear to the child. Furthermore, some children may misapply the idea of intentionality to illness situations. One child we treated strongly denied that she had caught a virus from another child who had exhibited the same symptoms a week earlier: "Susie is my friend," she stoutly explained. "She wouldn't make me sick by giving me a virus."

The preoperational child also has a very concrete understanding of language. This characteristic can result in miscommunication of medical information (Whitt, Dykstra, & Taylor, 1979). Consider, for example, children who jump to conclusions when the physician mentions the use of dye ("die") or diabetes ("die of betes").

Young children's immature understanding of the body may also predispose them toward horrifying notions such as bleeding to death when one is punctured during a blood test (Sheridan, 1975). Similarly, the idea that the way to heal is to remove something is reasonable to a tonsillectomy patient but was terrifying for one child with a vision problem, who believed his eyes would be removed during eye surgery (Petrillo & Sanger, 1972). The pediatric psychologist's ability to anticipate and interpret such beliefs can help dispel such frightening misconceptions.

Psychosocial Development

Clearly, a knowledge of normal cognitive development is essential to the practice of pediatric psychology. However, the child's cognitive development is only one aspect of the child's growth. This section explores the child's development of a sense of self.

The earliest conceptualization of psychosocial development to influence both pediatrics and psychology was Freud's stage theory. Some of the first studies on children's fears in medical settings were based on concepts such as castration anxiety, which were drawn from psychosexual formulations. Similarly, early descriptions of children's coping focused on analytically postulated processes such as "intellectualization" versus "denial." Although still applied in some branches of psychiatry, Freud's theory is not frequently used today in medicine and psychology.

Erik Erikson's psychosocial model parallels many of Freud's concepts, but it focuses more on developing strengths and skills than on psychopathology. Many pediatric psychologists view Erikson's theory as a useful description of early development (e.g., Willis et al., 1982). Although Erikson's theory describes adult development as well, we will focus here on his ideas about the developing child.

In Erikson's first stage, labeled *basic trust*, the newborn develops from an egocentric, dependent organism to an 18-month-old toddler with the beginnings of social sensitivity and independence. The newborn is aware only of fluctuating needs such as temperature regulation, contact comfort (a dry diaper), and hunger—and of the satisfaction of those needs. The infant at this time is genetically equipped with the ability to emit signals that elicit the caregiver's attention and affection (Levine, 1980; Murphy, 1974). Only after several weeks does the infant begin to associate need reduction with the primary caregiver, who comes to symbolize a safe haven in which needs are satisfied and pain is alleviated. Because of this association, the infant of several months develops separation anxiety or psychological distress when parted from the caregiver. Fear of strangers follows from this identification of the primary caregiver as the object of trust.

During the basic trust period, the infant also begins to actively manipulate the environment, and, as a toddler, becomes more skilled at locomotion. Locomotion allows the young child to follow the caregiver and to maintain contact if the caregiver moves away. At the end of this stage, awareness of concepts like object permanence makes it easier for the child to endure times when the caregiver is temporarily out of sight.

The second stage, labeled *autonomy*, describes the push toward independent manipulation of the world in the child from 18 months to 3 years of age. Not only do the child's motor responses allow for more independence, but the ability to fantasize and the sense of self as separate from the caretaker contribute to the child's autonomy. The use of language enables the child to make requests and exert more control over the environment. Oppositional behavior (often labeled the "terrible twos"), in which the child invokes the word "no" a great deal and tests parental limits, demonstrates the child's need to define the appropriate parameters for behavior. During this time, the child comes to take responsibility for bowel and bladder functions and for feeding.

The third stage, referred to as *initiative*, finds the 3- to 6-year-old child further engaged in self-definition. By this time, the child should have acquired a variety of social skills, including the ability to elicit positive adult attention and assistance, and to interact effectively with peers. Taking turns, leading as well as following, and competing in a nonthreatening fashion are important components of social competence at this stage (White et al., 1973). Physical appearance and typical bodily functions become focal points; children identify themselves with their bodies. Also, sexual identification with the same sex parent occurs, and a strong sense of personal goals and identity develops.

In the fourth stage, which Erikson called *industry*, the 6-year-old to preteen child's sense of self and regulation of behavior shows the impact of individuals outside of the home. The influence of school and peers becomes clearer. The child also focuses on acquiring academic, social, and motor skills in these contexts, and the view of self is highly colored by the ability to succeed in these areas.

Finally, in *adolescence*, Erikson's fifth stage, the child utilizes his or her new logical ability to build a set of values that differ from parental values. The development of a sense of self, which has been ongoing since birth, becomes the central theme of this stage. Answering the question "Who am I?" is the goal, and many differing roles may be experimented with to ascertain their fit to the new self. The struggle for independence from parents, both physical and psychological, intensifies.

Theories of psychosocial development argue that, although children of all developmental levels share basic concerns for such matters as contact with parents and physical integrity, the basic internal tasks of each stage differ. The pediatric psychologist's ability to determine which tasks have yet to be accomplished and which goals have been reached is critical in choosing a developmentally appropriate intervention—for example, deciding to enhance the development of trust versus autonomy, facilitating sexual identification or a focus on academics, or diminishing the negative impact of injury or illness on the child's unique, developmentally specific sense of self.

Of course, even the most skillful intervention may not completely negate the disruptive influence that poor health and necessary medical treatment have on a child's cognitive or psychosocial development. Some of these potential disruptions are considered next.

Impact of Medical Problems and Treatment on Development

The extent to which cognitive or psychosocial development may be retarded by injury, illness, or medical intervention is unknown, as is the degree to which appropriate intervention can mitigate these effects. However, it is logical to assume that stress, discomfort, and removal from the natural environment to a medical environment are likely to have some negative impact on a developing child. Karoly (1982) noted that, in the past, chronically ill children have been viewed as "the inevitable victims of a downward spiral," in which an early disruption continues to limit further growth. He argued that an adaptational view would conceive of illness only as a *potential* threat to health-related competence and that this threat might be overcome. *Vulnerable* to *resilient* patterns in children (Murphy & Moriarty, 1976) reflect the range of impact an event can potentially have on a child. Especially vulnerable children may be strongly affected by a minor stressor, whereas resilient children are relatively unaffected even by major stressors. Such processes are worthy of much further research. Before the pediatric psychologist can empirically examine these processes or clinically engineer appropriate coping, however, likely threats to normal development must be identified.

To an infant, the most serious threat to psychosocial development posed by illness or injury is a weakening of the developing bond between the infant and a consistent caretaker (Bowlby, 1982). Injury or illness may disrupt the attachment process (Willis et al., 1982) both because of separation of child and caretaker and because a caretaker may be reluctant to become firmly attached to a seriously ill infant. Naturally occurring interactions such as rocking, cuddling, and being spoken to both stimulate and soothe the infant. Barowsky (1978) suggests that deprivation of such interactions can result in the infant's intellectual and emotional impairment. Abstract cognitive-emotional tasks in older infants, such as the development and resolution of separation anxiety, may be delayed as well, resulting in a tenuous development of trust and a delay in autonomous functioning.

Indeed, one of the most common problems seen in toddlers who are physically ill is regressive behavior, including dependency, babytalk, and clinging to the caretaker (Willis et al., 1982). Temporarily being denied the chance to locomote and to make choices may also cause increased oppositional behavior or may result in the abandonment of the process of autonomy. Overprotectiveness on the part of the caretaker can exacerbate such problems (Magrab & Calcagno, 1978). The child's view of self may also be confused or distorted because the integrity of the body so strongly influences self-concept at this age (Willis et al., 1982). Finally, separation anxiety can be intensified rather than resolved at this time. Robertson (1958) described a sequence of reactions that very young children hospitalized for the first time had when separated from their parents. First, the children cried inconsolably. Then they lapsed into despair, acting withdrawn and depressed. Finally, they appeared to have adjusted but demonstrated an unusual and unexpected detachment from parents and caretakers when reunited, which in some cases took months to resolve.

The school-age child who is just acquiring a set of skills relevant to academic, social, and motor functioning and who is hospitalized must deal not only with parental separation, but also with separation from roles such as playmate or student, which are of increasing importance. The desire and ability to accomplish new skills may subsequently be diminished (Magrab & Calcagno, 1978). The interaction with peers necessary to gaining appropriate social skills may be lacking. Furthermore, a child who is perceived to be odd or different because of illness may be ostracized upon returning to school and the playgroup. (The impact of illness on academic skills and peer interactions will be considered in more depth in chapter 3).

Finally, the ill or injured adolescent faces the trials of normal adolescence with an additional source of stress. The desire for independence from parents may be denied; parents are likely to increase rather than decrease their control of the adolescent because of the illness (Peterson, 1972). Furthermore, the adolescent is likely to be well aware of any illness-imposed dependence and to resent it (Willis et al., 1982). Concerns about physical appearance, natural at this stage, may be intensified by illness or disfiguring medical treatments. Some adolescents may have doubts about their sexual abilities or their ability to find employment (Magrab & Calcagno, 1978), and limitations in contact with peers and with members of the opposite sex reduce social skill development, particularly the development of dating skills.

We have not systematically described interventions to prevent these disruptions in psychosocial development because little is currently known about how best to promote resiliency in the face of such trials. However, pediatric psychologists often profitably employ interventions such as self-control training for anxiety and academic skill building (e.g., Meichenbaum & Goodman, 1971). In particular, interventions focused on the family, ranging from decreasing separation anxiety in the toddler to enhancing independence in the adolescent, seem important, as do treatments to build social skills and methods to promote peer contact. Whatever interventions are designed, they must take into account the impact of multiple systems on the child; these systems are described in detail in chapter 3.

Chapter
Three

Systems
Considerations in a
Pediatric Population

Early conceptions of illness, injury, and treatment largely ignored the influence of systems outside the child in influencing adaptation and outcomes. Acknowledgment that the ill child does indeed function within multiple systems is an important facet of work in pediatric psychology that distinguishes the field from other types of behavioral medicine. These systems, which influence the child and which the child in turn influences, include the family, peers, and school.

THE FAMILY

In the last 15 years, several organizations dedicated to the interests of the families of ill children have been formed. The best known of these are Children in Hospitals (founded in 1971) and Parents Concerned for Hospitalized Children (founded in 1972). These organizations underline the need to consider the many ramifications of the ill or injured child's role in the family. They also exemplify the more active role families now assume in the care of their hospitalized children.

This increased familial responsibility for the child begins at conception with prenatal care and intensifies at birth. We will first consider parent-infant interactions in the newborn period. As will be seen, mere parent-infant physical contact during this period is vitally important to later development. For the ill or injured toddler or child of elementary school age, parental contact during periods of hospitalization can also be critical. Therefore, we will next consider the literature on the influence of parental presence on the hospitalized child. Following that discussion, the importance of intervention with the entire family rather than just the child and the use of family therapy techniques in pediatric interventions will be briefly considered. The impact on ill or injured children of family factors such as parental attitudes and problem-solving skills is then described. Finally, we will consider the influence of the ill or injured child on the other family members. These topics merely sample the possible issues pertaining to family involvement in pediatric psychology.

Parent-Infant Contact

In the last 2 decades, clinical and developmental psychologists have increasingly emphasized the importance of early parent-infant interactions. The attitudes of physicians and other medical staff toward the postpartum period have also changed. No longer are mothers encouraged to remain inactive and to have contact with their infant only during feeding. Instead, most hospitals encourage mothers to assume full care of their infants from the time of birth, with nursing staff acting as consultants or teachers rather than as primary care agents for the child (Magrab, Sostek, & Powell, 1984). The importance of maximizing contact between the mother and her infant has been underlined by a number of investigators (Klaus & Kennell, 1982; Trause, 1981). Extensive contact with infants from the time of birth on increases maternal confidence and diminishes anxiety (Sostek, Scanlon, & Abramson, 1982). Given opportunities for extensive contact, fathers interact with their newborns very much as mothers do (Parke & O'Leary, 1976); this fact suggests the importance of early contact for fathers as well.

Both in the first few days following birth and later in infancy, interactional difficulties such as poor parental or infant responsiveness or parental insensitivity to the infant's cues, negative affect, or lack of interest can signal problems (Ainsworth, Blehar, Waters, & Wall, 1978). This observation is particularly true for infants with low birthweight, who are more likely to be neglected or abused (Elmer & Gregg, 1967; Klein & Stern, 1971). The pediatric psychologist can assist in recognizing early interactional difficulties and in counseling parents about methods of dealing with the infant. Field (1977, 1982), for example, described infant-adult *interaction coaching*, in which parents acquire information about appropriate methods of responding to their child. Having parents observe a professional giving the Brazelton Neonatal Assessment Scale, with its differing techniques for soothing or stimulating the child, has also been shown to be valuable (Widmayer & Field, 1980).

For infants at risk for later psychological problems and cognitive deficits, a variety of interventions may be important. Helping parents achieve appropriate developmental expectations and counseling against overprotection that can disrupt normal development (Lewis, 1979) may reduce later problems. Coordinating the work of specialists in nursing, nutrition, speech and hearing, and social work may be necessary (Magrab et al., 1984). Kass, Sigman, Bromwich, and Parmelee (1976) suggest that frequent multidisciplinary follow-ups are likely to lead to strong parent-child attachment and optimal child development. Most importantly, parents need to receive training in appropriate follow-through activities for home use with the infant (Bricker & Bricker, 1976).

All of these interventions focus on maximizing the positive influence of parent-infant contact. As noted in chapter 2, the importance of the parents' physical contact with the child diminishes as the child develops. However, for the ill or injured child in the relatively foreign medical setting, the mere physical presence of family members assumes a renewed importance.

Family Presence for Young Hospitalized Children

Peterson, Mori, and Carter (1985) suggested that attitudes toward family presence have gone through a series of stages. In the first stage, parents were banished from the pediatric ward and allowed only weekly visits. Next, professionals began to argue that the mother should be allowed to accompany the child. Gradually, the less sexist word *parent* was employed, and the child's bond to both mother and father was stressed. Currently, pediatric psychologists suggest that the ill child should not be separated from the family; the parents and siblings as a system are regarded as important for the hospitalized child's emotional well-being.

The concept that an ill child should not be removed from the family is not a new one. A report made to the British Parliament in the 1700s stated, "If you take away a sick child from its parents or its nurse, you break its heart immediately" (quoted in Schaffer, 1967, p. 34). However, it was common medical practice to do just that until fairly recently. In the 1950s, the Platt Committee on the Welfare of Children recommended to the British government that all mothers be allowed to room-in with their children (Roskies, Mongeon, & Gagnon-Lefebre, 1978). The first study on parent rooming-in, also conducted in Great Britain, documented improved hospital adjustment in children whose mothers were allowed to room-in (Brain & Maclay, 1968). However, hospitals were slow to change policy. It took hospitals in the United States 2 decades to allow maternal rooming-in. In the mid-1950s, most New York hospitals allowed parental visitation for only 2 hours a week, whereas, by the mid-1970s, 54 percent of the general hospitals and 83 percent of the pediatric hospitals in New York allowed parents to remain continually with the child (Hardgrove, 1980). From the mid-1950s to the mid-1970s, the number of general hospitals allowing rooming-in increased tenfold, and the number of pediatric hospitals allowing this arrangement increased fivefold (Azarnoff, 1976). By the end of the 1970s, some pediatricians were stating categorically that "no child should be put in a hospital setting that will not let a parent remain overnight" (Gabriel, 1977, p. 525). Some physicians even argued that the parent should remain with the child in the operating room until after anesthesia induction (e.g., Mason, 1978).

There are a variety of advantages to parental rooming-in, especially for young children, who are at the most risk for later problems (Douglas, 1975). Separation anxiety can be diminished, communication with the child can be facilitated, and the child's sense of control over events can be enhanced (Peterson et al., 1985). The essential element of trust is strengthened by parental presence (Mason, 1978). This trust is particularly important in a very young child, who may not otherwise retain during a prolonged separation the concept that the parent still exists to provide care (Koocher, 1984). Normal discipline and family practices can be maintained as well, making the hospital experience less discontinuous from "real life."

Even with improved hospital policies, many parents still do not choose to room-in (Prugh & Jordan, 1975), and thus parental separation remains a major stressor for hospitalized children (e.g., Goslin, 1978; Schrader, 1979). There are a variety of likely explanations for failures to room-in. In our experience, parental work schedules, lack of child care for other siblings, and lack of information about the stress of separation all influence this decision. In a series of interviews conducted a year after hospitalization (Peterson & Shigetomi, 1982), parents reported the single most stressful event for the child had been remaining alone in the hospital overnight. This factor was rated as more stressful than vomiting blood postsurgically, receiving injections, or undergoing venipunctures. Characteristically, one parent commented that, if she had been aware of how upsetting remaining in the hospital alone would have been for her child, she would have made arrangements to stay. Because the hospital in this study allowed but did not encourage rooming-in, many of these child patients were subjected to unnecessary stress. Therefore, one important part the pediatric psychologist can play is providing parents with information about the stressful nature of separation prior to hospitalization so that necessary child care and employment adjustments can be made.

Some evidence suggests that emphasizing the importance of parental presence and describing the role the parent can play in the child's medical care increase the amount of time parents spend with their children during hospitalization. Roskies et al. (1978) demonstrated that weekly meetings designed to encourage parents to spend time with their hospitalized children resulted in a slight increase in the number of visits (82 percent of possible occasions after intervention versus 77 percent before intervention) and a greater increase in the amount of time spent with the child (55 percent of the possible time after the intervention versus 36 percent before the intervention). The role a pediatric psychologist might play in arranging increased family contact as well as the value of providing free babysitting or housing near the hospital (such as that provided by the Ronald McDonald Houses) are important topics for future research.

Although the data clearly indicate that parental visitation and rooming-in are valuable to the hospitalized child, it is not obvious that parental presence is a positive influence in all medical situations. For example, dentists strongly prefer that parents not be present during dental procedures (Gershen, 1976), perhaps because their anxiety can increase the child's fearfulness. Venham (1973) reported that mothers often verbalized their fearfulness, covered their eyes, displayed exaggerated facial expressions of fear, and emitted fearful noises in front of the child about to undergo dental work. It is easy to see why such provocative behavior would be unwelcome in the dental suite and how appropriate parental training by the pediatric psychologist could be useful. Specifically, parents might be cautioned that their fearful verbalizations, gestures, and expressions can provoke the child's fear. Helping parents decide whether they are able to remain relaxed and encouraging or whether they may wish to absent themselves is a first step. If parents wish to remain, the goal of training would be to assist them in coping internally with their child's discomfort while supporting the child externally. *Stress-inoculation techniques* such as relaxation, deep breathing, and cognitive self-instruction could be used to bolster internal resources. In addition, role playing and modeling of supportive interventions by the pediatric psychologist could also increase parents' positive responses toward the child.

Data also suggest that children are more likely to cry and complain during an invasive medical procedure if a parent is present than if the parent is absent. Gross, Stern, Levin, Dale, and Wojnilower (1983) observed children during blood tests, and Shaw and Routh (1982) observed children's reactions to injections. Both studies concluded that children emitted more distress behavior in the presence of their parents, but both also argued that this did not indicate that the parents were a source of distress. Rather, Shaw and Routh suggested that the parents simply facilitated the expression of anxiety, which the children experienced whether or not the parents were present. They argued that the expression of distress was not necessarily a negative outcome; not expressing distress might be more negative.

Gross et al. (1983), on the other hand, hypothesized that the children's behavioral manifestations of fear accelerated in the presence of the parent. In a child's typical encounter with the world of bumps and bruises, they suggested, the parent usually intervenes to stop a noxious stimulus. When the parent fails to intervene, the child may increase the visible signs of upset to elicit the usual parental response. This pattern of behavior resembles an *extinction burst*, or the temporary increase in frequency or intensity that commonly accompanies the removal of a particular behavioral reinforcer (in this case, parental attention and assistance). Perhaps ensuring that the parent clearly understands the inadvisability of intervention to halt the procedure would help in this situation.

Other data show parental presence as having contradictory effects (e.g., Venham, Bengston, & Cipes, 1978; Vernon, Foley, & Schulman, 1967), sometimes increasing and sometimes decreasing children's distress; still other studies indicate that parental presence at a crucial time, such as during anesthesia induction, can have overall positive effects (Bush, Melamed, Sheras, & Greenbaum, 1986). A variety of factors may contribute to the mixed conclusions of these studies. Age of the child, type of preprocedure preparation employed, demands of the particular medical procedure, and prior experience may all contribute to a child's reaction (Peterson & Mori, 1988). Melamed and Bush (1985) also suggest that the characteristics of the parent-child interaction influence the child, with anxious parents exacerbating distress and parents who are effective copers ameliorating distress. (Such parental characteristics will be considered in more detail in the section on family factors.)

Gross et al. (1983) also argued that, although some parental behaviors could elicit child distress, parents prone to such behaviors should be taught more appropriate and effective means of coping rather than be banned from the procedure. As will be seen next, a growing literature supports the merit of this suggestion.

Family-level Interventions

Treatment directed toward the family as well as the child should be the rule rather than the exception in pediatric psychology. Such interventions may range from training parents to cope with a discrete medical procedure, as advocated by Gross et al. (1983), to intensive family therapy.

Peterson and Shigetomi (1981) attempted to teach parents a general method of helping their children adjust to stressors involved in minor elective surgeries. Four treatment groups were employed. Two of the groups of children and their parents received training in three types of coping skills: visual (visual imagery was suggested), linguistic (appropriate self-talk was engineered), and kinesthetic (cue-controlled slow breathing and deep muscle relaxation were employed). Parents were told they were to serve as their children's therapists, cuing the children as to when to employ particular coping techniques and assisting them in correctly performing the coping behaviors. In addition, one of the coping skills groups and one of the other groups not receiving coping skills training viewed a film of a child model reacting adaptively to a minor surgery. In general, children and parents who had received the coping skills training showed less distress both before and after surgery. This outcome was particularly marked on measures of parental self-report. During invasive procedures such as blood tests, children who participated in both the coping and modeling conditions showed less behavioral distress and were more cooperative than children in the other three groups. A year after receiving the coping skills training, a third of the parents reported generalizing its use beyond the hospital to other stressful situations (Peterson & Shigetomi, 1982).

Meng and Zastowny (1982) provided additional evidence of the efficacy of teaching parents coping techniques. In this study, parents of prospective pediatric surgery patients viewed a film on stress inoculation procedures. Children whose parents viewed the film were found to be less stressed and more cooperative than children whose parents had not; in addition, parents who viewed the film reported less anxiety than those who had not. This study and others thus support the suggestion that parents can be taught to respond adaptively to children's invasive procedures and that such training limits both parental and child distress.

Other interventions have focused on teaching parents of chronically ill children the specific skills necessary for dealing with regimen compliance or medical interventions. Many chronic childhood disorders require frequent home-based treatments. Hemophilia, a disease characterized by dangerous bleeding episodes that can be triggered by trauma or occur spontaneously, is one example. Bleeding can be stopped in some children by the intravenous infusion of the blood factor the child is missing. This infusion can be done at home, reducing the cost and lifestyle disruption incurred by a hospital visit. However, if the infusion procedures are not conducted appropriately, the factor concentrate may lose its potency, the child's veins may be damaged, or infection may result (Varni, 1983). Thus it is essential that parents master the appropriate infusion methods and that children cooperate with the intervention.

Sergis-Deavenport and Varni (1982, 1983) described a highly detailed training procedure for parents of children with hemophilia. The training consisted of three stages. In the first stage, the factor replacement was reconstituted under sterile conditions using special bottled water. In the second stage, the syringe was prepared. In the third stage, the infusion was given and completed. There were 20 discrete behaviors in the first stage, 20 in the second, and 36 in the third. Training consisted of having the parents observe and rehearse the component behaviors of each stage until they could perform each behavior correctly over 80 percent of the time. Then parents went on to learn the next stage. In follow-up checks, the five parents taught to complete the replacement factor infusion in this fashion demonstrated over 97 percent accuracy in appropriate behaviors. Similar behavioral techniques have been used to assist parents and their children in diabetic insulin injection (Epstein et al., 1981), physical therapy for hemophilic patients (Varni, 1981a), and treatments for children suffering from cystic fibrosis (Stabler, Fernald, Johnson, Johnson, & Ryan, 1981). (Such treatments will be discussed further in subsequent chapters.)

Other interventions geared toward the family are less circumscribed and specific. For example, the pediatric psychologist may assist in delivering upsetting information, such as a diagnosis of mental retardation or terminal illness (Roberts & Wright, 1982) or may try to enhance open communication and continued development in a family with a seriously ill child (Spinetta et al., 1982). Providing emotional support and a chance for family members to examine and understand feelings is another important role (Magrab & Calcagno, 1978). Sourkes (1977) described four specific types of interventions for facilitating family coping, including enhancing communication, being available on an ongoing basis, explicitly "giving permission" for a parent to use the psychologist as a support, and modeling skills for parents to employ with the child.

Paradoxically, although most interventions by the pediatric psychologist are family-centered, family therapy as such has been used infrequently, although there are exceptions (e.g., Bauer, Harper, & Kenny, 1974; Lask & Kirk, 1979). Some well-known family therapists (e.g., Minuchin, 1974; Minuchin, Rossman, & Baker, 1978) have focused on child and adolescent pediatric problems such as asthma, diabetes, and anorexia nervosa. Minuchin's model describes the concepts of *boundaries* and *enmeshment*. In normal family functioning, boundaries are established that allow children to function independently, negotiate problems with siblings and friends, set goals, etc., while parents are progressively allowed to take less responsibility for the children as they develop. In families with an ill child, however, these boundaries can become blurred.

Because of the illness, some parents who might otherwise allow considerable independence may feel compelled to reassert control over common activities such as the child's selection of food, play activities, and dress. By contrast, enmeshed parents may feel a particular need to be in control to a degree independent of the illness. In other words, they may use the illness as an opportunity to ignore the child's actual abilities. This in turn can create difficulties in marital, parent-child, and sibling relations as the ill child receives preferential treatment. Thus families with a medically ill child may be particularly prone to family dysfunction—and amenable to family therapy.

Training in family therapy, as well as regarding the family as the unit of analysis, is likely to be very beneficial to the pediatric psychologist of the future. Some pediatric psychologists have suggested that, from diagnosis onward, a series of interventions focused on the entire family should be executed (Gogan, O'Malley, & Foster, 1977). Planning family interventions would require knowledge concerning the manner in which a variety of family factors influence the developing child. This is an area in which very little research has been conducted, though recently a small number of researchers have begun investigations.

Family Factors

One of the factors mentioned in the previous section on family presence for young hospitalized children is the role parental anxiety might play in exacerbating a child's distress reaction to an invasive medical procedure. Bush et al. (1986) observed children and their parents during the waiting period in an outpatient clinic. They found that children's crying and fear-related verbalizations were positively related to observable parental agitation and anxious reassurance of the child. Children's crying and complaining of fear were also related to parents' self-reported anxiety and fear. Parental distraction of the child, in contrast, was correlated with less crying and fewer verbalizations of fear. These results suggest that an ill-prepared parent can have a detrimental effect, whereas a well-prepared parent can have a more positive effect on a child's coping. In addition, it is undoubtedly the case that an anxious child elicits parental upset and concern, just as an upset parent increases a child's anxiety.

Parental beliefs about appropriate child behavior and preparation can also influence children's coping behaviors. For example, Heffernan and Azarnoff (1971) interviewed mothers and their children separately prior to a medical clinic visit. They classified mothers as either suppressive ("It is not OK to cry") or nonsuppressive ("Crying when hurt or upset is OK"). They found that suppressive mothers were simultaneously less likely to be aware of their children's anxiety and more likely to have a highly anxious child. There was an interesting interaction between level of preparation, anxiety, and curiosity about the medical procedure. If the child had asked for preparatory information, detailed information from the mother resulted in less anxiety than did scant information. However, if the mother had initiated the discussion, minimal information was related to lower levels of anxiety than was detailed information. It remains unclear whether anxious parents give their children more detailed "reassuring" information (which Bush et al., 1986, noted tends to provoke children's distress) or whether information that exceeds the children's interests or abilities is threatening. Peterson, Ridley-Johnson, Tracy, and Mullins (1984) focused on parents of elective surgery patients. They measured the parents' style of coping by using Rosenbaum's (1980) self-control scale and asked the parents about their typical method of preparing their children for dental or medical procedures. They also obtained parental ratings of the children's usual responses to medical procedures. Parents with high active coping scores gave their children more information prior to preparation than did parents with lower scores. The more information a child was reportedly given, the lower that child's ratings of upset behavior.

Parents' ability to cope with problems not only influences the short-term reactions of child outpatients and pediatric elective surgery patients, as has been described, but may also influence children's compliance with chronic disease regimens. Many authors have suggested that the psychosocial adjustment of physically or chronically ill children is strongly influenced by parental attitudes and reactions (e.g., Garrard & Richmond, 1963; Maddison & Raphael, 1971; Mattson, 1972). Parental ability to deal with the problems associated with chronic illness seems particularly critical. For example, Fehrenbach and Peterson (1983) found that the quality of problem solving demonstrated by parents of children with phenylketonuria (PKU) was strongly related to biochemical measures of the children's actual dietary compliance. In this study, parents responded to vignettes in which they were asked to solve a problem involving their children's low phenylalanine diet. Mothers of children in good dietary control were able to formulate more and better solutions to both high and low stress problems.

Similarly, Kucia et al. (1979) examined problem-solving responses in families of children with cystic fibrosis. These children were rated by their physicians as being either poorly adjusted (having emotional, behavioral, or academic problems) or well adjusted. The families with the well-adjusted children had the most creative problem solutions. Kucia et al. suggested that such creativity is particularly important in allowing the family to be supportive of the arduous medical regimen of the cystic fibrosis patient. Finally, Hanson, Henggeler, and Burghen (1987) noted that family supportiveness was related to good metabolic control in young diabetes patients.

It seems clear that family factors can influence the acutely or the chronically ill child either positively or negatively and that the pediatric psychologist can exert some control over these factors by teaching skills such as problem solving and by enhancing family support. The focus of the discussion thus far has been on the impact of the family on the ill or injured child. The child in turn also affects the family.

Child Influence on the Family

Travis (1976) described a number of factors that determine the extent to which the child's medical condition may influence the family. Many of these factors have to do with aspects of the disease itself, such as the need for complicated special diets (diabetes, asthma, kidney disease, PKU) or housecleaning (asthma). Some have to do with physical costs to the parent, such as sleep disturbance (asthma, hemophilia) or fatigue from giving physical therapy (spina bifida, cystic fibrosis, muscular dystrophy). Financial costs of the treatment, wheelchair adaptations, or medical equipment also have effects. Finally, the emotional burden of living with an unpredictable medical disorder is very real.

The stress this burden places on a marriage can be significant. In many forms of chronic illness, the two parents often deal with the disorder in very different ways (Spinetta et al., 1982). The stress and disappointment of the child's illness and the focus on the child to the exclusion of the marital relationship can result in separation or divorce (Lansky, Cairns, Hassanein, Wehr, & Lowman, 1978). Unfortunately, the child's guilty notion that he or she caused the marital conflict—common in many well children following divorce—may be quite accurate in the case of the seriously ill child. The pediatric psychologist with skills in marital therapy may therefore often decide to concentrate on the marital dyad to the temporary exclusion of the child patient. At minimum, the pediatric psychologist should know the danger signs of a stressed marriage and be able to effect a referral for a couple needing this kind of assistance.

Siblings of the ill or injured child are also at risk. This vulnerability was graphically illustrated in an early study by Sipowicz and Vernon (1965), who examined the influence of hospitalization by using twin subjects in which only one of the twins was hospitalized. The nonhospitalized twin was studied in each case as a nonstressed control, but the authors reported that, in 20 percent of the twins, the nonhospitalized sibling was more distressed than the hospitalized twin. Clearly, these siblings were undergoing their own stresses: It is not uncommon for the stressed siblings of an ill or injured child to be enjoined to be "mature and generous" and not to make demands on the already "burned-out" parents (Spinetta et al., 1982). Siblings are likely to harbor a variety of emotions toward the ill or injured child, including both rivalry and guilt (O'Meara, McAuliffe, Motherway, & Dunleavy, 1983). Accordingly, the pediatric psychologist may need to view the sibling of a medically ill child as at risk (Goslin, 1978) and either intervene or arrange intervention for that child as well.

Viewing the ill or injured child as part of a family system is an important step. We have discussed many of these findings as if the effects were unidirectional, with a mother's anxiety eliciting agitation in the child or the ill child's medical condition causing guilt in a sibling. However, research in the future will increasingly examine reciprocal influences among family members. Some investigators are now arguing that pediatric psychologists should go even further, to a multisystems conceptualization based on Bronfenbrenner's (1979) ecological theory. This conceptualization considers the child in the context of multiple, interlocking systems. The most important system to the young child is, of course, the family. However, as the child advances in age and experience, other systems such as the peer group and the school increasingly influence development. Even though the pediatric psychologist does not usually have direct contact with these systems, it is essential that he or she be aware of their potential influence on the child. The role of the pediatric psychologist in reference to peers and school will be briefly considered next.

PEER AND SCHOOL SYSTEMS

Next to the family, peers are the developing child's most important source of attachment and social stimulation. Rewarding interactions with peers are also the primary vehicle for appropriate separation from parents and for gaining independence. Furthermore, the child's developing self-image is influenced by the sense of self reflected by peers.

Research attention to the peer system has developed only recently (e.g., Hartup, 1979, 1983). Sociograms and other popularity measures have been used for some time, but recent research has gone beyond identifying popular and unpopular children to describe *socially rejected, socially neglected, average*, and *popular* children. Socially rejected children are actively disliked and tend to be aggressive and uncooperative. Socially neglected children, on the other hand, tend to be neither liked nor disliked, but rather are ignored by peers. Average children make up the majority. They are neither as actively disliked as socially rejected children nor as widely selected as are popular children. They are well-liked by a small number of children and disliked by a still smaller group. Popular children are actively sought out by peers as partners in work or play.

Where does the chronically ill child or the child who has missed school due to acute injury or illness fit in? This question is a critical focus for future research in pediatric psychology. There are certainly many threats to the peer relationships of such children. Some investigators have found that peers negatively evaluate chronically ill children, apparently on the basis of the presence of the illness itself (e.g., Roberts, Beidleman, & Wurtele, 1981). Other investigators have discovered that disability or disfigurement does influence peer reactions but only for certain types of interactions (Harper, Wacker, & Cobb, 1986). Furthermore, the concomitants of many types of illness or injury—such as disfiguring burns or surgeries, hair loss, extreme weight loss or gain, and changes in facial structure secondary to steroid treatment—can make a child self-conscious and withdrawn. Finally, one of the primary characteristics of the rejected child is a deficit in socially competent behavior (Ladd & Mize, 1983). According to Hops and Greenwood (1981), what appears as a social skills deficit is often simply social behavior typical of a younger child. Social competence is customarily acquired through repeated rehearsal in daily play, and, if deprived of social opportunities just as these skills are rapidly developing, the child may remain at a lower developmental level than same-age peers. Avoiding a disruption of peer interaction is thus an important part of any psychosocial intervention for the hospitalized or homebound child.

Pediatric psychologists have suggested a variety of approaches to the problem of maintaining peer contact. In some forms of chronic illness, children attend camp with other ill peers. Seeing peers with the same illness participating competently in regular activities helps normalize and strengthen the ill child's self-concept (Primack & Greifer, 1977). Hospital playgroups (e.g., Thomas, 1980) or group therapy sessions for older hospitalized children (e.g., Gardner, 1977) can be important for building interpersonal skills, enhancing emotional support, and decreasing the sense of being different from other children (Drotar, Crawford, & Ganofsky, 1984). Social skills training accompanied by modeling, discussion of social skill building techniques, and role playing may also be useful. Some psychologists have even intervened with peers at school, preparing them for the physical changes in the child, discussing specifics of the disease and treatment, and answering their questions (Katz, Kellerman, Rigler, Williams, & Siegel, 1977). Because such interventions can have positive effects on some child peers and negative effects on others, evaluation of the influence of such interventions seems essential (Schroeder, 1979).

Although contact with neighbors and friends is likely to be important, the school is the primary social focal point for the child of elementary school age. Intervention with peers in the school system is thus extremely important. Especially for older children, peer reactions may be the part of school reintegration they fear most. However, the reactions of peers present only one part of the challenge that the pediatric psychologist must face in assisting the ill or injured child in reentering the school system. Many children who are or have been seriously ill fear any separation from family, whether for hospitalization or for school. School phobia is particularly prevalent among chronically ill children (Lansky, Lowman, & Gyulay, 1975). Family-centered interventions combined with an anxiety reduction treatment are often indicated for such children.

School is the equivalent for the child of an adult's vocation, and children who do not return to school may show the same maladaptive reactions as unemployed adults (Katz, 1980). Returning to school thus marks the equivalent of returning to full employment, to a complete and productive life (Cyphert, 1973). At times, parents of children with catastrophic illness may believe that requiring the child to continue to work toward a future that may never be actualized is futile. Nothing could be further from the truth. As Katz et al. (1977) have noted, "Denying the child the opportunity to engage in goal-oriented behavior can reinforce feelings of hopelessness and despair" (p. 72). Therefore, assisting parents in planning appropriate social and educational goals is vitally important.

At times, it is the teacher and not the parent who feels that educating a chronically ill child is wasted effort or cruel to the child. Spinetta et al. (1982) pointed out that convincing such a teacher that the child can learn and grow and that the teacher can contribute to normal development is an important task for the pediatric psychologist. Similarly, school-based intervention is needed for the teacher who is inappropriately using a double standard in which more demands are made of peers than of the ill or injured child. Still other teachers are too rigid, not allowing work to be made up even when the missed assignments are unavoidable products of clinic appointments or hospitalizations (Greene, 1975). Some school systems have also been resistant to special programming. For example, Ganofsky (1981) reported on a successful appeal to an Ohio board of education to allow renal patients on dialysis to get tutoring on dialysis days and to attend regular school the other 3 days a week.

Finally, there are teachers and other school officials who become anxious in the presence of a seriously ill or injured child. Some investigators have suggested that such anxiety is a product of the reminder, in the form of the child's illness or injury, of one's own vulnerability (Kaplan, Smith, & Grobstein, 1974). Concern that the child may become ill in class may also provoke anxiety (Drotar et al., 1984), sometimes prompting principals or teachers to refuse to allow such children to attend.

Crittenden and Gofman (1976) argued that school-based prevention should occur in a number of areas, including facilitation of the child's return to a normal school routine, management of the social stresses that accompany necessary medical regimens, and preventive advocacy with teachers and other school officials (including education centered on the special needs of the ill or injured child). Spinetta et al. (1982) suggested that the school has three essential needs when working with the ill or injured child: (1) accurate, specific medical information; (2) an awareness of the psychosocial implications of the child's condition for the child, the family, and the school; and (3) a referral source who is part of the health care team and willing to answer questions about the child as they arise. This listing provides a good definition of the role of the pediatric psychologist in patient-based school consultation.

In addition to interventions focused on specific children, there are other situations in which the pediatric psychologist may be involved in school consultation. Mesibov and Johnson (1982) describe such general school-based consultation for pediatric psychologists. This consultation differs from work done by school psychologists in several ways. School psychologists are a primary part of the school system. They are funded by the school system, and their responsibilities include assessment, placement, and programming for children within the school system. In contrast, the pediatric psychologist is more often based in an academic or medical setting and therefore more likely to approach the school system as an external agent with unique expertise. With the enactment of Public Law 94-142, the schools have been charged with supplying appropriate educational experiences for all ill, injured, and handicapped students. The pediatric psychologist's expertise in dealing with such children's strengths, limitations, and unique psychosocial and cognitive needs is valuable in planning such school-based programs. Many school systems need to develop routine ways of responding to children with special needs, and the pediatric psychologist can be instrumental in creating such protocols. Although individualized programming will always be needed, establishing a general set of procedures can go far in assuring that these children's needs are met.

To give just one example, a protocol for a child with newly diagnosed diabetes might include a conference with the teacher, principal, and other interested parties in order to dispel myths about the problem, answer questions, and give information. The child's special need for snacks, regular mealtimes, and a balance of exercise and food would be stressed. Provision would be made for urine or blood testing and for insulin injections at appropriate times of the day. The teacher would be taught to recognize insulin reactions or diabetic coma and to take appropriate actions. Psychosocial normalization of the child would be a routine part of the program, including the education of classmates as needed. Finally, the school system would be made sensitive to signs of stress, depression, and potential school withdrawal and would intervene as necessary to strengthen the child's coping resources. A checklist of such issues, with attached educational information and model plans for action, could be instrumental in implementing the protocol.

This section concludes the description begun in chapter 1 of pediatric psychology as an emerging discipline. We have discussed several factors that help characterize the field: its historical development; the special experience of work within medical settings; need for sensitivity to the child's developmental stage; and focus on the child's place in family, peer, and school systems. In our attempt to define the field, we have already begun to describe the pediatric psychologist's primary roles and duties. In chapter 4, we extend this description with an overview of the many different types of intervention currently used in pediatric psychology.

Chapter Four

Differential Role of Psychological Interventions

Comprehensive coverage of the many different psychological interventions employed in pediatric medicine exceeds the scope of this book. The following chapters will therefore only sample from the various types of interventions characteristic of pediatric psychology. These methods of intervention have been organized according to their relationship to traditional psychological interventions and medicine. Specifically discussed in this chapter are traditional psychological problems coincidentally occurring in a medical setting, psychologically caused medical problems, and psychosocially caused medical problems. Chapter 5 offers an examination of psychological interventions for medical problem management, and chapter 6 describes psychological interventions to reduce medically caused distress. These five topic areas will be presented as if they were nonoverlapping, but we should explicitly acknowledge at the outset that a problem can have both psychological and organic etiologies and that intervention for a problem may thus belong in more than one category. Cognitive, emotional, social, and physical factors all undoubtedly contribute to the majority of problems seen in children. Furthermore, it is true that diversity in the stresses, experiences, levels of social support, and coping abilities in children suffering from any given disease may be as great as the diversity among those same elements in children suffering from different diseases (Stein & Jessop, 1982). The organizational scheme of the following chapters is used only to group similar techniques together loosely, not to define discrete areas of cause or treatment.

To give precision to some of our discussions, we will refer to diagnostic criteria spelled out in the fourth edition of the *Diagnostic and Statistical Manual of Mental Disorders* (DSM III-R; American Psychiatric Association, 1988). Although this diagnostic system has certain limitations in terms of reliability and validity, especially with regard to child diagnoses, it is useful because it is a commonly used and readily available source of symptom definition.

PEDIATRIC PAIN AND PSYCHOLOGICAL INTERVENTION

To begin our discussion of pediatric targets for intervention, we will describe a single pediatric problem that spans all five of our defined areas: the serious but underresearched problem of pediatric pain (Varni, 1983). Although pediatric pain assessment and management have been the subjects of increasing research in the last 5 years, the large majority of studies on pain have been conducted with adults, and definitive information on the measurement and treatment of children's pain awaits further research (Beales, 1982). Hospitalized children tend to receive far fewer medications for pain than do adults (Beyer, DeGood, Ashley, & Russell, 1983), even when the pain they experience is thought to equal that of adults (Perry & Heidrich, 1982). Common and apparently unfounded beliefs exist among medical staff that children do not experience pain to the same extent as adults and that they recover from pain experiences more quickly (Eland & Anderson, 1977). The diverse etiologies and meanings of pain responses in children make researching the topic all the more difficult.

Pain Accompanying a Traditional Psychological Problem

A traditional psychological problem of school phobia or withdrawal reaction may be accompanied by complaints of pain, typically headache or stomachache. Because follow-up of children showing such symptoms often reveals that many may actually have an organic basis to their complaints (Routh, Ernst, & Harper, 1988), it is important to have a medical work-up completed prior to instituting a behavioral intervention. If no physical findings appear in the examination or at follow-up, the problem is best considered as a behavioral excess, to be eliminated via extinction and replaced by adaptive behaviors that are modeled, shaped, and rewarded in a classic pattern of behavior modification (Bandura, 1969).

Pain as a Psychological Problem

A more serious form of psychopathology exists when psychological difficulties precipitate medical problems. One such problem, Somatization
Disorder, or Briquet's Syndrome, is defined in the DSM III-R as at least 13
recurrent and multiple somatic complaints beginning before age 30 and
for which medical attention has been sought but no physical basis can be
found. Ernst, Routh, and Harper (1984) suggested that many children
who are hospitalized for abdominal pain actually suffer from Somatization
Disorder, which apparently can begin in childhood. The basic presentation of children showing precursors of Somatization Disorder involves
seeking out medical attention for a growing list of physical problems for
which no organic bases can be found. Affective difficulties or reactions to
stress seem to be translated directly into physical ailments. After a time,
the child becomes identified with the "sick role," and a primary vehicle
for familial support becomes responsiveness to the complaints of illness.
Ernst et al. (1984) reported that children whose parents sought out a
physician due to the child's abdominal pain reported only 1.95 other
symptoms at first but that this number grew rapidly. Children presenting
with pain duration of less than 1 year had 2.21 symptoms, whereas those
with complaints of abdominal pain over a year's duration had 4.04 symptoms. Such data suggest an escalation of the disorder in childhood that is
characteristic of the adult form of psychopathology, in which a progressive number of physical symptoms evolve from what is apparently an
environmentally based psychological problem.

Clearly, this characterological disorder in children requires treatments different from traditional behavioral methods. Because other family members often show the same forms of psychopathology (Routh &
Ernst, 1984), systems level interventions are often indicated. Establishing
a new role for the child, who has come to view himself or herself as ill or
as an invalid, is a special challenge. If the child can become invested in a
healthy student, playmate, or other adaptive role, progress is more likely.
The child also needs to acquire more adaptive ways of eliciting support
from others and dealing with stress. Because of its complexity, this type
of intervention is likely to involve continuing psychological care after
discharge from the hospital.

Pain as a Psychosocial Problem

Psychosocial problems leading to medical problems include those disorders in which a parent or other member of the immediate family plays
the major role. Pain in children that is precipitated by child abuse is an
example of such a systems-related problem. Physical abuse is considered

in greater detail in a later section of this chapter. For the present, we will consider an unusual subset of abuse, that of Munchausen Syndrome by Proxy.

Munchausen Syndrome, now labeled *Factitious Disorder with Physical Symptoms* by the DSM III-R, describes a series of behaviors in which individuals subject themselves to potentially harmful medical treatments to create the symptoms of physical illness. In 1977, Meadow added the words *by Proxy* to this diagnostic category to indicate illnesses in children that are the product of deliberate acts by the parent. Cases have included poisoning (Clark, Key, Rutherford, & Bithoney, 1984), adding blood to urine to mimic hematura (Outwater, Lipnick, Luban, Ravenscoft, & Ruley, 1981), and physically induced apnea (Rosen et al., 1983). In reviewing 19 cases of Munchausen Syndrome by Proxy, Meadow found that in each case the mother was responsible for the abuse. Typically, the father in the family was distant and uninvolved, and the mother was extremely attentive and attached to the child. Chan, Salcedo, Atkins, and Ruley (1986) described a case of Munchausen Syndrome by Proxy in which the child's gastrointestinal pain and vomiting was the result of poisoning by the mother. (Chan, the pediatric psychology intern working with the child, diagnosed the case.) Chan et al. suggested that pediatric psychologists should screen for Munchausen Syndrome by Proxy in cases where there is physical disease that does not respond to normally effective treatment, in which the child recovers quickly whenever hospitalized, and in which the mother shows unusual closeness to the child but little apparent concern for the illness or for the potential detrimental effects of the child's and mother's isolation from the father and siblings. Screening requires careful questioning of all of the child's caregivers, looking for patterns of illness consistent with parent-based causation, testing the child for drugs that might produce the current symptoms, collecting on-site blood or urine samples that might otherwise be tampered with by the parent, and even isolating the child from the parent for a test interval if necessary.

Pain Due to Existing Medical Problems

In some cases, rather than physical symptoms appearing for psychological or psychosocial reasons, psychological problems appear secondary to necessary physical interventions for existing physical disease. One area where this often occurs is in the treatment of juvenile rheumatoid arthritis. This affliction typically begins under age 10 with swelling and stiffness in the joints. The knees and elbows are most affected, and the disorder can be both painful and crippling. Treatment involves medication, exercise, and wearing of splints to reduce the crippling effects on the joints (Jette, 1980). Because the exercises and splint wearing are uncomfortable, even painful, noncompliance is a frequent problem. Rapoff, Lindsley, and Christophersen (in press) reported that rewarding a 7-year-old victim of systemic onset juvenile rheumatoid arthritis with tokens improved the child's compliance. Frequency of wearing wrist and knee splints at night and lying prone on a firm surface (to prevent hip contractures) during the day increased from near 0 percent of the prescribed occasions to 80 percent of the prescribed occasions. As will be seen later, similar techniques can be effective for increasing other types of compliance.

Pain Due to Medical Treatment

At times, the pain that is the target for the pediatric psychologist comes not from the disease but from the medical intervention itself. Such pain is increased by both anxiety and uncooperativeness. As one example, treatment of serious burns often necessitates extremely painful and distressing interventions such as tanking and debridement. In these procedures, the child is placed in a tub of warm water and any dead tissue is removed by scrubbing with sterile gauze. The pain and fear this creates in the child can result in extreme withdrawal or combative behavior, which can prolong the treatment and aggravate the child's medical condition. The negative affective and behavioral side effects of such medical treatment are often reduced by psychological treatments such as hypnosis (Bernstein, 1965) or reward systems that reinforce apparent coping and build self-confidence (Varni, Bessman, Russo, & Cataldo, 1980).

Most of the interventions considered above are not unique to pediatric psychology but are drawn from behavioral, clinical, and community psychology. However, the methods of assessment, treatment decisions, implementation, and follow-through techniques are specific to the challenge of this particular setting. Most have evolved through a combination of the clinical and research pressures described in chapter 1. The purpose of this overview has been to describe their broad scope as well as their important commonalities, which will now be examined in more detail.

TRADITIONAL PSYCHOLOGICAL PROBLEMS UNRELATED TO MEDICAL CONDITIONS

In his chapter entitled "Pediatric Psychology as an Area of Scientific Research," Routh (1982) outlined a large range of research contributions made by pediatric psychologists. Not surprisingly, most of the areas he outlined demanded traditional psychological expertise and only coincidentally appeared in a medical setting. These research areas included assessment of developmental status and child behavior problems, primary prevention, treatment of behavior problems, parenting skill training, intervention with high-risk infants, and treatment of child abuse and neglect. Investigations of treatment techniques included counseling, behavior therapy, and family therapy. In fact, there are few problems that might appear in a general child assessment or intervention text that are not applicable to the practice of pediatric psychology. To limit the focus of the present chapter, we will sample from four types of common pediatric psychology problems that illustrate traditional clinical child referrals often occurring in medical settings. These include (1) academic dysfunction due to learning disability or mental retardation, (2) "Dr. Spock" referrals (regarding common childrearing problems), (3) behavioral problems mistaken as medical problems, and (4) traditional behavioral or developmental problems coincidentally occurring in hospital settings.

Academic Dysfunction Due to Learning
Disability or Mental Retardation

Some strictly psychological problems are initially thought to be secondary to the child's medical condition. Consider, for example, the chronically ill child who also has a learning disability. Chronically ill children are frequently perceived by their pediatricians to have nonspecific intellectual problems (Korsch, Cobb, & Ashe, 1961). Some forms of illness can even induce learning disabilities (Wright, 1972). On the other hand, a preexisting learning disability or motivational problem unrelated to the child's medical condition can cause academic difficulties (Pless & Pinkerton, 1975). These academic problems can then be mistakenly attributed to missed school, medication side effects, or the illness itself. This misattribution is potentially serious because it blocks appropriate remediation of the problem. Routh (1978) has argued that, because children with specific learning disabilities require a select system of educational tools and techniques for remediation, it is essential that the causes of academic difficulties be correctly identified where they exist. Consider this example:

> Angela was a 7-year-old girl who was being held back in first grade for the second time. She had a rare blood disorder that required frequent hospitalization, and thus she had missed over 40 percent of existing school days in the last 2 years. Angela's parents were inclined to be overprotective, making few demands

of her, especially during her periods of hospitalization. Angela did not yet recognize the letters of the alphabet, although she could recite them. Similarly, when presented with her first-grade workbook, she did not recognize numbers nor understand basic relationships such as bigger and smaller or same and different. Angela's teacher and parents attributed her poor skills to her illness and frequent absences from school. It was only after the consulting pediatric psychologist observed Angela draw a distorted human figure (used in this case to assess self-esteem and concept of self and others) that testing for learning disabilities was considered. Angela was found to have visual-spatial dyslexia, a learning disability characterized by distorted and immature visual perceptual abilities. A special remedial program for her allowed her to move into second grade (albeit with continued special help) the next year.

Intellectual and perceptual assessment skills are also necessary in cases where academic dysfunction is due to retardation rather than to the existing medical condition. Mental retardation occurs at a higher frequency in children with certain physical problems, such as heart disease and leukemia. Because these children already require services from the medical community, pediatric psychologists often become involved in school placement recommendations (Magrab & Lehr, 1982). Decisions that may have been put off because of a medical crisis frequently are considered only as the child is being discharged from the hospital. Knowledge of intellectual testing procedures, as well as of special tests for assessing social maturity and motor abilities, is essential. (See chapter 2 for further discussion of these techniques.)

"Dr. Spock" Referrals

Another type of referral is seen in what have been termed "Dr. Spock" or "one hand on the door" questions (Wright, 1979). These questions are typically asked of a physician after a well-child visit or after minor medical treatment for an unrelated illness. As the parent exits, with one hand on the door, he or she asks about some common childrearing problem. Consider the following example:

The mother of 4-year-old Stephen had brought him in to his pediatrician's private practice office because of a minor ear infection. Stephen was examined, and a prescription for antibiotics was written. Stephen's mother received the prescription, thanked the physician, and then added, almost as an afterthought, "There is one more thing I have been wanting to ask you about. Stephen is still sucking his thumb, especially at bedtime or when he gets nervous. My mother-in-law says to put pepper on his thumb to get him to stop, but that seems cruel. What would you suggest?" The physician, who had three other families waiting, was in a difficult position. "Ignore it and he will outgrow it" was an acceptable suggestion given the high frequency of spontane-ous remission of thumbsucking, and such advice would save time. On the other hand, it ignored the potentially dangerous effects of putting pepper on the thumb, possible detrimental effects of thumbsucking on the child's teeth, and the very real possibility that the behavior signaled the need for more exten-sive assistance. The problem was not solvable in 2 or 3 minutes. It was a "no-win" situation.

Roberts and Wright (1982) have suggested that the pediatric psy-chologist can assist the physician in preparing a protocol for "hand on the door" childrearing questions. They recommend a variety of books for general parenting (e.g., Christophersen, 1977; Patterson & Gullian, 1968) and for specific problems such as divorce (e.g., Salk, 1978) or obesity (Silberstein & Galton, 1982; Stuart & Davis, 1972). The physician might also choose to refer the parent's question to a psychologist for more extensive discussion and assistance. Schroeder and her colleagues have described a call-in/come-in consultation service that was offered by several pediatricians for 2 hours a week (Schroeder, 1979; Schroeder, Goolsby, & Stangler, 1975). During that time, parents could obtain answers to basic psychological or behavioral questions. Difficulties requiring more intervention were handled in a more extensive appointment.

Behavioral Problems

A related problem is seen in parents seeking assistance for common childrearing problems they perceive as having medical causes but that are really learning or behavioral problems. Nocturnal enuresis, or wetting the bed at night, is an example of such a problem. Enuresis is defined by the DSM III-R as an involuntary or intentional voiding of urine onto one's clothing or bedding that occurs at least twice a month in children ages 5 to 6 years and at least once a month in older children and that is not due to a physical disorder. Nocturnal enuresis is the most common type. It is estimated that 15 to 20 percent of 5-year-olds, 5 percent of 10-year-olds, and about 2 percent of adolescents suffer from nocturnal enuresis (Lovi-bond & Coote, 1970). In treating the problem, many physical factors should be considered and ruled out, including structural problems and infection. In addition, ethnic and socioeconomic factors and the nature and type of toilet training may play a part.

Because behavioral treatment of nonorganic enuresis is typically quite successful, it is unfortunate that in some cases children are first treated with medication (most commonly imipramine, brand name Tofranil), which can have such negative side effects as cardiac arrhythmia (Lake, Mikkelsen, Rapport, Zavadil, & Kopin, 1979) and disturbances in sleep and mood changes (Doleys, 1979). In addition, imipramine can be lethal in relatively low doses (Walker, Milling, & Bonner, 1988). Making behavioral strategies available to parents and supplying professional backup when needed is an important charge for the pediatric psychologist. As the following discussions illustrate, ongoing consultation, encouragement, feedback, and reprogramming where necessary are essential components of a successful behavioral program.

There are many commonsense methods of dealing with enuresis, such as periodic awakening of the child (which is mildly successful) and fluid restriction (which is relatively unsuccessful). The two most effective behavioral interventions are the Mowrer bell and pad (see Doleys, 1977) and Dry Bed Training (Azrin, Sneed, & Foxx, 1974). The bell and pad operates via a pad that, when contacted by even a drop of urine, triggers an alarm, thus awakening the child. It is unclear whether the pad operates, as was initially believed, through classical conditioning, in which awakening is paired with a full bladder, or through a punishment paradigm, in which wetting is consequated by a rude and noisy awakening. The large majority of children treated with the bell and pad become continent after several weeks of training. However, the apparatus must be set up correctly and used consistently. Consistent use can be a real problem because the parents and siblings are often awakened by the alarm while the enuretic child sleeps blissfully through it, having to be awakened by a parent. For these reasons alone, it is very helpful to have a professional assist the family in maintaining appropriate and consistent use.

Azrin et al. (1974) used the bell and pad as one part of an intensive intervention for enuresis. This program, called Dry Bed Training, employs reinforcement for keeping the bed dry, training to encourage sensitivity to a full bladder and control over retention, and overcorrection in the form of rehearsing restitution (cleaning up self and the bed) and appropriate toileting. In this program, the child is periodically awakened and asked if he or she needs to urinate. If the bed is already wet, the child performs a drill consisting of rehearsing appropriate voiding behavior; replacing wet bedsheets with clean ones; and dressing in clean, dry pajamas. This drill is repeated up to 20 times per incident. If the bed is dry, the child is praised and asked to use the bathroom. Later in training, the child who reports needing to urinate is asked to hold the urine for an hour, thus affording practice in bladder control. This relatively arduous method is highly successful, particularly when implemented by a professional. Parents in consultation with a professional can also be very successful, as a case we treated recently indicates:

> John was a 7-year-old boy who had been wetting the bed three to four times a week for as long as his mother could remember. His mother, a registered nurse, sought help for him because she was reportedly at the end of her rope. As she remarked, "I can't get up every morning and bathe him, change the bed, do a wash, and still make it to work on time."
>
> The mother received careful instruction in some of the components of Dry Bed Training. John was allowed to drink a good deal of his favorite fruit drink before his 8 o'clock bedtime. Between 9 p.m. and 1 a.m., his mother woke him every hour and inquired whether he needed to urinate. The first night, he urinated appropriately at 10 p.m. and midnight and was dry all night. The next night, he reported not needing to urinate at 9 and 10 p.m. and at 11 p.m. was wet. He was sent to the bathroom for voiding practice, and when his mother checked him 5 minutes later, she found him asleep on the bathroom floor. (Difficulty in awakening is often reported in cases of nocturnal enuresis.) She washed his face with a cold washcloth, and this behavior was subsequently added to his drill. He would enter the bathroom, attempt to urinate, wash his face with cold water, return to his room, change pajamas and bedsheets, place the wet pajamas and sheets in the washer, return to bed, get up, enter the bathroom, etc. Initially, he protested repetitions of the drill, but when his mother held firm, he sleepily repeated the drill eight times.
>
> He had only two more wet incidents, and, after 10 days, his mother reported that he was arousing himself to urinate before her midnight check. After 2 weeks, there were no more wet nights, and his mother gradually dropped the periodic awakenings. She was delighted and reported, "After all these years, I couldn't believe it was so easy."

Although not all parents will regard the multicomponents of Dry Bed Training as easy or have such quick success, nocturnal enuresis is a problem commonly presented to the pediatrician and one that is usually readily amenable to intervention by the pediatric psychologist.

Behavioral or Developmental Problems in Hospital Settings

This last category includes traditional psychological problems appearing coincidentally in medical settings. These difficulties are clearly behavioral or developmental but, because they occur in the hospital setting, involve the pediatric psychologist. Noncompliance, temper tantrums, and aggression are common child behavior problems. These can be merely annoying at home but often seem intolerable in the crowded, stressful environment of the pediatric ward, as seen in the following example:

> Derrick had been very ill, but now he was feeling like himself again. Because of the need for continued IV medication and the climate at home, which provided little support, it was necessary for him to remain in the hospital for a few additional days. The understaffed nursing personnel were having a terrible time dealing with him. He began by getting out of bed and investigating the room as far as his IV leads would take him. He would forget and go too far, however, and had twice knocked the IV stand over; had pulled the needle loose, causing infiltration under his skin; and had kinked the tubing. Giving him a portable IV unit resulted in his crashing down the hall, with the unit bumping into walls and other patients. When confined to bed again, he responded by deliberately pulling the IV out at every opportunity.
>
>   A change in environment was suggested by the pediatric psychologist; more toys and a videocassette recorder to play cartoons instead of daytime dramas helped to reduce his disruptive behavior. Next, token rewards contingent on proper care of the IV unit were instituted; this measure was found to be effective in decreasing his noncompliance and overactivity.

For most such problems, common operant procedures such as reinforcement, shaping, time-out, and extinction are very effective. In many cases, the pediatric psychologist is involved in constructing a behavioral program that nursing staff, hospital volunteers, or parents then actually administer. Recently, Tarnowski, Kelly, and Mendlowitz (1987) conducted a study of nurses' reactions to several behavior modification programs commonly used by the pediatric psychologist. They found that programs to accelerate behaviors (e.g., praise or a token system) were preferred over reductive techniques (e.g., extinction or time-out) and that nurses were more favorably disposed toward programming for more serious disorders (e.g., aggression) than for less serious problems (e.g., mild tantrums). Interestingly, how ill the child was (e.g., anemia versus leukemia) did not influence the nurses' judgments. In addition to investigating treatment effectiveness, research examining the reactions of personnel who will be required to implement the pediatric psychologist's programs is important: It does not matter how effective techniques might be if they are not used as planned.

Interventions as Teamwork

The pediatric psychologist can greatly extend his or her influence by ensuring that programs are used appropriately. The literature on training nurses (e.g., Rapoff, Christophersen, & Rapoff, 1982) and parents (e.g., Petrie, Kratochwill, Bergan, & Nicholson, 1981) in pediatric settings to deal with behavioral problems and improve children's learning is a relatively recent, extremely crucial facet of pediatric psychology. Because a variety of staff persons—including lab technicians, child-life workers, physicians, and nurses—can either enhance or destroy the effectiveness of a behavioral program, enlisting the help of relevant personnel and providing necessary background and guidance for them is essential. Staff must be fully informed concerning any program being used with a child and given a rationale for the program and information concerning ways in which they can support it.

A few examples from our own work on presurgical preparation may help illustrate this process. We often teach children to deal with invasive procedures by making the necessary part of their bodies available to the health care agent, closing their eyes, breathing deeply, relaxing their muscles, and focusing on a visual image or self-statement. A laboratory technician who loudly asks, "What is wrong with this kid; is he going to faint?" when the child closes his eyes and begins to breathe deeply; a nurse who insists on tightly restraining a child who is relaxed and coping well during an injection; or a child-life worker who urges a child to work out anger over a procedure with which there has been little difficulty all undermine the teaching program. The informed laboratory technician can say, "I see you are closing your eyes to get ready for the blood test and taking slow, deep breaths. Good for you, that will help!" The nurse can allow the child to relax during the injection without restraint and praise the child's cooperation, and the child-life worker can assess the degree of self-efficacy in the child's response to the procedure prior to assuming that the procedure has been emotionally traumatic. Staff persons can be supportive if they are fully aware of and willing to cooperate with the preparation program.

The problems that have been discussed in this section are referred to psychologists because they fall within the traditional parameters of psychological treatment. They are referred to a *pediatric* psychologist because the child with the problem is concomitantly receiving medical care or because the parents have sought out medical intervention for a clearly psychological problem. Our next section deals with a different sort of problem. This problem is initially manifested as a medical disorder but is found to have psychological origins. Although psychosomatic problems are also within the purview of traditional psychological interventions, there is often some family resistance to psychological intervention for such cases.

PSYCHOLOGICALLY CAUSED MEDICAL PROBLEMS

Recurrent pain in children is a common reason for contacting a pediatrician or other specialist. Oster (1972) estimated that, in a general sample of schoolchildren, 14.4 percent reported recurrent abdominal pain, 20.6 percent reported recurrent headache, and 15.5 percent reported specific leg or arm pain ("growing pains"). The majority of each of these pain types were judged as psychogenic in origin. An emotional or psychological etiology does not imply that the pain is not genuine or that the child is malingering. In many such cases, the pain is real and debilitating. However, parents and children often rebel against a psychogenic explanation because they fail to understand that *psychological* does not mean imaginary or fictitious. Green (1967) quoted a typical parental reaction: "One thing I know, it's not mental. That boy has real pain!" (p. 85). Furthermore, the attitudes of some physicians toward Chronic Recurrent Abdominal Pain are signified by the acronym CRAP, which they use to describe the disorder (Walker, 1979). Needless to say, this orientation fails to facilitate psychological intervention.

Of course, reports of chronic pain necessitate a search for organic disease. It is unfortunate that a search revealing nothing often nevertheless involves procedures that are uncomfortable and dangerous to the child. Hughes and Zimin (1978) noted that medications, medical tests, and surgeries often complicate rather than alleviate chronic pain reports. Despite such potential complications, it is typically necessary to perform at least the noninvasive tests for common child disorders before hypothesizing a psychological base. As Hughes and Zimin have remarked, "A conspicuously meticulous physical examination has important psychotherapeutic value in patients with recurrent abdominal pain. Even if the history does not suggest an organic lesion, the physician, child, and parent need to be satisfied as to the absence of abnormal physical findings" (p. 87).

As was noted earlier in this chapter, chronic abdominal pain in childhood is one of the most common precursors of Somatization Disorder in adulthood. The pain is typically reported to be erratic and unrelated to activity or eating. It is described as cramping or a dull ache commonly lasting from 5 minutes to 3 hours (Stone & Barbero, 1970).

Children with abdominal pain often appear depressed and are seen as mature for their age but dependent on the parent. The accompanying parent is typically described as being anxious and excessively concerned over the child's well-being (Hughes, 1984; Hughes & Zimin, 1978). Such characteristics have usually been regarded as etiological. However, a child who does not have strong peer contacts at school and play because of frequent illness, who must rely upon the parent for an alleviation of pain, seems likely to develop an unusual dependency on the parent. Similarly, a parent who cannot relieve the child's pain is likely to be distressed and to focus on the child's health. It is not surprising that some physicians have noted that the child and parent often develop a sense of helplessness with regard to the pain (Stone & Barbero, 1970). The following case example illustrates this problem:

> Samantha was an attractive 10-year-old girl with recurrent abdominal pain of 3 years' duration. Samantha's father was a salesperson with a large firm whose job necessitated much travel. Samantha's mother had been working as a computer programmer but was on the verge of losing her job because of absences to stay home and take care of Samantha. Samantha's pain could (and did) come on at any time of day, necessitating a sudden stop to all daily routines. Samantha described the pain as a radiating, aching sensation slightly to the left of center of her abdomen. Her mother reported that "Sammy" was such a good girl, she did not cry or complain but just lay on the couch "all doubled up with big tears rolling down her face." Her mother supplied a heating pad and distraction; nothing else seemed to help.
>
> Samantha had experienced a range of tests, including a guaiac test for occult blood in the stool, a barium enema, a proctoscopic examination, and an intravenous pyleogram, all with negative findings. Her mother still had the haunting feeling that something serious, even potentially fatal, had been missed, but, as she put it, "It doesn't seem there is anything left to do." Samantha never received a medical diagnosis for the cause of her pain.

One finding that does seem to be a clearly causative rather than reactive factor is a positive past family history of chronic pain (e.g., Green, 1967; Routh et al., 1988). Children with chronic abdominal pain and their families reportedly experience more life events related to illness and hospitalization than do either families with a behaviorally disordered child or healthy families (Hodges, Kline, Barbero, & Flanery, 1984). Hughes and Zimin (1978) may have summarized families with chronic pain best by noting, "With these families, the use of bodily sensations, physical explanations, and medical or surgical procedures to deal with psychic distress is a way of life" (p. 573). Thus intervention to decrease chronic abdominal pain must logically focus on relearning methods of dealing adaptively with dependency needs, social and academic challenges, and other stressful life situations. The pediatric psychologist may need to focus on the entire family or on the child-parent dyad rather than on the child alone to deal with such chronic pain.

There is very little in the literature describing successful treatment of children with abdominal pain. Sank and Biglan (1974) successfully used self-monitoring and reinforcement for decreased pain reports to treat a 10-year-old boy with a 2½-year history of recurrent abdominal pain. In a later study, Miller and Kratochwill (1979) demonstrated the effectiveness of time-out for pain behavior in treating a 10-year-old girl with a 1-year history of abdominal pain. Sanders et al. (in press) recently described a multicomponent program in which children were taught to self-monitor pain and use relaxation training and parents were instructed to ignore pain and selectively attend to well behavior. Of children receiving this treatment, 87.5 percent were pain free at the time of a 3-month follow-up. In addition to these treatment methods, family therapy, relaxation, and distraction techniques are commonly used. Additional research in this area is an important challenge for the pediatric psychologist.

Chronic headache in children shows some interesting similarities to, as well as differences from, recurrent abdominal pain. Difficulties in diagnosis are similar, which is noteworthy because recurrent abdominal pain is typically dealt with by internists, whereas pediatric headache patients are most often seen by neurologists. To date, there have been no reliability studies on identification of children with recurrent headache (Hoelscher & Lichstein, 1984), and the absence of standardized assessment devices in this area is striking (Andrasik et al, 1982). Like parents of chronic abdominal pain patients, parents of pediatric headache patients are inclined to avoid psychogenic explanations, although they are more sympathetic to the notion of environmentally based etiologies such as stress. Child headache sufferers, like children with chronic abdominal pain, often have relatives who report the same affliction (Jay & Tomasi, 1981). Investigators have posited a social learning influence in some cases and a genetic predisposition to headache in others (Brown, 1977). In general, the medical literature on headaches has not focused on personological or familial characteristics of child patients, and the extent to which headache is believed to have organic versus behavioral or environmental bases is unclear. Fewer than 15 percent of chronic headaches treated by neurologists are found to have a clear neurological basis (Hoelscher & Lichstein, 1984). Behavioral treatments have been equally or more effective than pharmacological treatments (Ramsden, Friedman, & Williamson, 1983), thus suggesting that the psychological contribution to many headaches is substantial.

Over a dozen recent studies have now documented the utility of behavioral methods for reducing the frequency of children's headaches (Hoelscher & Lichstein, 1984). In one such study, Labbé and Williamson (1983) used a multiple baseline across three pediatric patients diagnosed as having migraine headaches. They examined the efficacy of finger skin temperature biofeedback and found that, at the end of treatment and at a 2-year follow-up, the children had completely eradicated their headaches by using the biofeedback techniques twice daily and at the first sign of onset. Although most studies have not shown such dramatic success, the use of relaxation techniques and biofeedback appears very promising.

Similarly, Ramsden et al. (1983) recently demonstrated the value of contingency management procedures with a child who was experiencing migraine headaches. This child was rewarded for witholding reports of head pain, first at home and later at school, on a DRO (differential reinforcement of other behavior) schedule. After several weeks of such rewards, the reinforcers were faded from daily to weekly and eventually discontinued. Ten months after the treatments were discontinued, the child showed continued absence of headache pain.

Of the differing types of headache, migraine may be the most debilitating to the patient and confusing to the diagnostician, and thus it most often has been the subject of treatment research. Athough there are fewer treatment studies of other headache types, it would seem logical that headaches that are more clearly psychogenic, such as chronic scalp muscle contraction headaches (i.e., tension headache—see Jay & Tomasi, 1981), would be even more amenable to behavioral methods, as this case history suggests:

> Erica was a bright junior high school student who presented with recurrent bilateral headache pain in the absence of neurological signs. Her headaches usually occurred toward the end of the school day and lasted for several hours. Lying down in a dark room and taking aspirin were typically effective in alleviating the pain. However, Erica was involved in several reportedly enjoyable after-school activities, which she had to miss whenever she had a severe headache.
>
> An interview suggested that Erica found lunch periods very stressful because she had not formed any close friendships and dreaded sitting alone in the cafeteria. Often, she studied in the hall during the lunch hour rather than enter the cafeteria alone. Her first class after the lunch break was biology, a difficult sub-

ject for Erica, particularly when lab work necessitated social exchanges and close visual tasks using a microscope or magnifying glass.

Erica was treated with some social skills assertion role plays and homework assignments that allowed her to acquire some lunchtime companions. She was also taught deep muscle relaxation, concentrating on her shoulder, jaw, and scalp muscles. She utilized the techniques for 3 minutes during each classbreak from late morning until the end of the day. Erica was seen four times over an 8-week period. She cancelled her fifth session because she had not had a headache for 3 weeks. She promised to return should the headaches resume, but she felt confident she had them under control.

Successful interventions for pediatric patients with headaches have been the focus of research for only the past 5 years. Much more work needs to be done in this challenging area. Some researchers have even suggested the possibility of teaching behavioral skills as preventive techniques, focusing on children who do not yet report headache pain but who have a positive family history (Hoelscher & Lichstein, 1984).

The etiological significance of a positive family history is clear for many psychosomatic disorders of childhood. Our next section focuses on a set of disorders that is even more clearly related to the family and the home environment.

PSYCHOSOCIALLY CAUSED MEDICAL PROBLEMS

In psychosocially caused medical disorders, an agent external to the child bears direct and primary responsibility for the child's medical condition. Not surprisingly, this agent is often one or both of the parents. We noted earlier in describing pediatric psychology's need to focus on the family that parental responsibility for caring for the child begins at conception and intensifies at birth. In the case of infants with nonorganic failure to thrive (NOFT), the parents are unwilling or unable to meet this responsibility effectively. Postulated causes of NOFT involve both psychological and emotional factors. In some cases, the parent is too disturbed to care for the child; in others, the parent is unaware of the appropriate way to care for the child, or there is an ongoing pattern of interactions in the family that prohibits appropriate care (Roberts, 1986). Regardless of which causes are implicated, the result is an infant who appears younger than chronological age, both physically and behaviorally. The infant is often listless and withdrawn and is sometimes incorrectly labeled as mentally retarded, although later assessment indicates age-appropriate intellectual abilities (Drotar, Malone, & Negray, 1980).

Like psychosomatic illness, psychosocially caused medical conditions often initially present as physical disease. Roberts and Horner (1979) described intervention for an infant with NOFT, beginning with the hospital admission. The child's primary problem was weight loss, so tests were run to rule out malabsorption and the child's diet was checked. Tests for diarrhea included stool cultures and urinalysis. A psychological consultation was requested to assess the infant's developmental level and the mother's potential depression. Because findings indicated the mother to be seriously depressed and no organic cause for the child's weight loss, follow-up at home to treat the mother's emotional disturbance was arranged.

It is often possible to predict which parents are most likely to have children with NOFT. A history of neglect or abuse in a parent's own childhood is one of the primary predictors (Altemeier et al., 1979), along with unemployment, illness, arrests, and evictions (Gaines, Sandgrund, Green, & Power, 1978).

In addition to background variables and family demographics, family stability and daily interaction patterns are related to NOFT. Erratic and unpredictable feeding habits are typically present. A mother who is not responsive to the infant or prepared for feedings because of her youth; her emotional, cognitive, or psychiatric dysfunction; or her substance abuse is typical. At times, responsibility for the infant is passed to a sibling or is shared among several adults, none of whom assume primary care. When the actual living habits of the family are probed, the reason for the child's failure to thrive can become quite clear:

> Mitsy was a tiny 5-month-old infant who appeared more like a newborn. She weighed only 11 pounds, a mere 5 pounds more than when she was born. She would lie very still in her hospital crib, sucking her fist, eyes unfocused. She was unresponsive to the nurses who fed her, rarely vocalized or cried, and, when she did cry, she was difficult to console.
>
> The psychologist learned from the division of social services that Mitsy's mother, Valline, had been abandoned by her own mother when she was 3 and raised by her maternal grandmother. Valline still lived with her grandmother when she was not staying with the man who had fathered Mitsy. This latter relationship was very unstable; the man was suspected of dealing in drugs, and Valline, although not physically addicted, often used a variety of drugs. Valline's grandmother took care of Mitsy while Valline was at work or with friends.

In interview, the psychologist determined that the grandmother was only 58 but showing distinct symptoms of Alzheimer's disease, with confusion, agitation, and memory loss. Both the grandmother and Valline claimed attachment to the infant and resisted any suggestion of out-of-home placement. Yet it was clear that neither person was currently capable of giving Mitsy the care she required. It appeared from interviews with both women that there had been times when there was no infant formula in the house and the grandmother had been puzzled at her inability to soothe the crying infant. It was not surprising that routine medical tests revealed that organic pathology was not responsible for the baby's failure to thrive. Mitsy was discharged to the care of her mother, but social services began an investigation that ultimately resulted in Mitsy's placement in a foster home, where she showed a rapid weight gain and increases in responsiveness.

Although this case had a "happy ending" for the infant, not all children are so fortunate. NOFT cases are often referred too late in the hospital stay to allow complete assessment of either the child or the family situation (Drotar, Benjamin, Chwast, Litt, & Vajner, 1982). Because some physicians view their task as ruling out organic disease rather than isolating the cause of the child's problem, arranging for psychological services in the community following hospital discharge is frequently neglected (Drotar, Malone, Negray, & Dennstedt, 1983). The recent development of services for psychological consultation to pediatric infant divisions (e.g., Drotar & Malone, 1982) demonstrates a sensible alternative. Here, infants with symptoms congruent with NOFT can be seen routinely and the families interviewed early in the hospital stay. Out-of-home placement is only one alternative treatment when NOFT is identified as environmentally based. Marital therapy, support arranged from relatives or volunteer agencies, substance abuse treatment, and parent education are all services that can be supplied by the pediatric psychologist to treat NOFT.

Child abuse is another psychosocially caused problem, and, like NOFT, it can present as being caused by an organic problem or accidental injury. In other situations, someone outside the home such as a school official or neighbor reports the abuse to an agency, which in turn arranges emergency room assessment by a multidisciplinary team that may arrange for hospitalization (Helfer, 1975). At least in the short run, the latter situation is in the child's best interests because it guarantees that some investigation will actually take place. Although physicians and other medical officials are often required to report cases of suspected child abuse, in many states no penalty is imposed for not reporting.

Furthermore, special diagnostic skills are required to distinguish accidental injury from abuse. Both a knowledge of the signs of abuse and the ability to focus the physical examination and recording of medical history on a search for those signs are needed. Not all medical personnel obtain training in these skills. Finally, evidence exists that there is less reporting (not necessarily incidence) of abuse within middle- to upper-class families and by private practice physicians (Light, 1973).

The effects of abuse on children can be grave. The Center for Improvement of Child Caring (1977) suggested that 50,000 children a year die from child abuse. Serious brain damage and neuromuscular problems are found in 25 to 30 percent of children who survive the abuse (Martin & Rodenhoffer, 1976). Abuse dwarfism (hyposomatotropism) is also seen, with impaired growth, delayed puberty, and intellectual retardation—all reversible if the child is removed from the abusive home (e.g., Money, 1977). There are a variety of potential psychological symptoms as well, including temper tantrums, aggressiveness, lack of impulse control, and distorted moral reasoning (Fontana, 1973; Reidy, 1977; Smetana, Kelly, & Twentyman, 1984). Lowered self-esteem, depression, and difficulty in forming trusting relationships may also result (Kazdin, Moser, Colbus, & Bell, 1985; Kinard, 1982). In fact, the physical wounds resulting from abuse may heal far more rapidly than the psychological damage:

Six-year-old Tabatha presented at the emergency room with a broken arm, which her mother reported occurred while the child was playing on a swing. The resident contacted the on-call psychology intern when the X-ray of Tabatha's arm revealed an earlier fracture of the wrist. The resident confided to the intern that, given the time (it was 10 p.m.), the story about the swing seemed unlikely and that the mother had been very evasive about the child's previous medical history. In interview with the mother, the psychology intern found her to be a young, unemployed single parent who had been drinking. She was indignant about having to speak with a psychologist and noted that the child was "always getting hurt, falling off things, and all like that." She wanted the arm treated and to go home and go to sleep. She claimed that the child had no regular pediatrician and had been seen in the emergency room on only one other occasion, for a torn ligament in her shoulder. (A deeper probe later revealed that this was accurate, for this hospital. The child had been seen at several other emergency rooms, however. The broken wrist had been set at a hospital across town.)

Tabatha was a wary child, small for her 6 years. She was initially very resistant to talking with the intern and said she did not recall the injury but that it must have happened "while I was playing." A physical exam revealed bruises in various stages of healing over her upper arms and back. She also denied memory of these injuries. When admitted to the hospital over the protests of her mother, she settled into her room rapidly and began watching television. She showed no problem separating from her mother. Throughout her stay in the hospital and initial placement in a foster home, Tabatha showed a striking ability to disengage from the adults who cared for her. She did not ask for her mother, nor did she appear attached to her foster mother. The superficiality of her interactions was frightening in so young a child.

The pediatric psychologist can assist in both the diagnosis and treatment of abused children. Familiarity with the physical and behavioral manifestations of abuse is necessary. A parent who has "shopped" for medical care at multiple locations, who is evasive about past medical care, and whose explanations for current injuries are vague deserves an in-depth interview. Such parents are often willing to talk about their own stressful life situations and how difficult their children are to handle. This beginning can lead to discussion of disciplinary practices the parents experienced as children. Although not always the case, many abusive parents themselves experienced severe discipline amounting to abuse (G.J. Williams, 1978). Often a parent does not even recognize such harsh discipline as abuse and lacks other child management skills.

The psychologist can also be instrumental in the treatment of abuse. Being available to the child for reassurance and communication is valuable, and it may be even more important to be supportive of the abusing parent. Spinetta et al. (1982) noted that "while the medical team members are attending to the child and while the child-protective team have as their obligation to bring the law to bear on the abusing parent, there is no one left to respond to the parent's very real cry for help" (p. 180). They argue that few parents deliberately set out to harm their children. Most have low self-esteem, unrealistic expectations of the child, a low anger threshold, or confused beliefs about discipline that result in abusive behavior. Because most children will ultimately be returned to the abusing parent, it is in the child's best interests for the parent to receive sympathetic and consistent assistance. This may require that the pediatric psychologist work through feelings of anger and repulsion at an individual who would physically harm a small child.

There is very little good literature on successful treatment of child abuse. Like most psychosocially caused problems, individual therapy for the direct perpetrator is likely to be helpful but insufficient in and of itself. Crisis intervention and 24-hour availability may be necessary (Beezley, Martin, & Alexander, 1976), and treatment of the parent-child dyad, the entire family, or the ecological system may be preferred to individual therapy (Brunk, Henggeler, & Whelan, 1987). Several past investigators have suggested group therapy over individual therapy (e.g., Feinstein, 1964; Paulson & Chaleff, 1973) because of the abusing parent's need for perception checking and peer support. Some group therapy formats involve multimodal treatment such as parent education, behavior modification, transactional analysis, and relaxation training (e.g., Justice & Justice, 1976). Self-help groups such as Parents Anonymous, CALM (Child Abuse Listening Mediation), and HELP (Home Emergency Lifeline for Parents) can be very helpful to some parents. Finally, the availability of a drop-off center for the child when the parent feels out of control seems essential (Kempe & Helfer, 1972).

The pediatric psychologist can be involved at any of these levels, from diagnosing the disorder, serving as a patient advocate, and performing individual therapy to arranging group therapy or actually leading it, and even to setting up community organizations or drop-off centers. Because there is almost no controlled treatment research in this area, contributing to scientific investigation of intervention methods would seem a critical charge for the pediatric psychologist.

Many pediatric psychologists consider prevention rather than remediation of child abuse to be their most important obligation. Early recognition of those at risk is the first step. The use of homemaker services to diminish disorganization in a disrupted household, to serve as a positive model, and to reduce isolation from the rest of the community has often been suggested (G.J. Williams, 1978). As we noted earlier, frequent, positive contacts with the infant and the encouragement of the parent-child bond can reduce later problems (Willis, 1976). Early education in child psychology and parenting skills also seems valuable.

Public education is an overlooked but important new charge, especially since the 1977 Ingraham versus Wright Supreme Court ruling allowing corporal punishment in the schools. Legitimizing violence against children can only encourage abusive practices in the home. Surprisingly, some states have conflicting laws regarding child abuse in the home. For example, Texas has a law against child assault, but the Texas Penal Code stated in 1974 that "the use of force, but not deadly force, against a child younger than 18 years is justified: (1) If the actor is the child's parent or stepparent . . . (2) when and to the degree the actor reasonably believes the force is necessary to discipline the child" (pp. 22-23). In such a setting, the pediatric psychologist may make important contributions through political action. In sum, by definition psychosocial problems require more than individual psychological intervention; intervention at each possible level can be instrumental in eradicating abuse.

We have considered three kinds of problems that are psychologically based but are often found in medical settings: traditional psychological problems unrelated to medical conditions, psychologically caused medical problems, and psychosocially caused medical problems. Pediatric psychologists also frequently deal with behavioral problems stemming from the medical setting itself. The next chapter considers problems that are primarily medical in origin. Treatment of these disorders relies on the pediatric psychologist's expertise in altering behavior to manage the child's physical disease.

Chapter Five

Psychological Interventions for Medical Problem Management

     A very large number of techniques could be considered in a discussion of the pediatric psychologist's contribution to managing physical disorders. These techniques include intervention methods commonly used by clinical child psychologists, such as reward systems, shaping, and self-monitoring; skills employed by behavior therapists, such as biofeedback, relaxation, and cognitive coping techniques; and interventions drawn from nursing and medicine, such as methods of injection, turning in bed to protect an incision, and exercise to prevent the crippling side effects of some disorders. These techniques differ greatly, and most are applicable to a variety of medical conditions. Rather than attempting a comprehensive discussion of all these methods, we have selected as examples four medical areas that demand very different intervention techniques. These include diabetic regimen adherence, seizure control, management of acute and chronic pain related to hemophilia, and the naturalistic coping strategies used by child asthma patients. The management of these disorders yields a sense of the diversity of techniques used within pediatric psychology.

DIABETIC REGIMEN ADHERENCE

Insulin-dependent diabetes mellitus has one of the most challenging and demanding medical regimens of all pediatric disorders. Diabetes is a chronic disorder of the body's ability to metabolize carbohydrates due to inadequate pancreatic release of insulin. The immediate result of the absence of insulin is a high level of sugar in the blood. Early symptoms include weight loss (because the body is unable to use the sugar in the blood), extreme thirst, frequent urination, weakness, and fatigue. If the child's diabetes is not diagnosed and treated, acidosis can develop. The child becomes progressively more dehydrated, with the skin and mucous membranes feeling dry to the touch. Eventually, if the child is not treated, coma and death can result.

The diabetic regimen involves a complex process of balancing the amount of insulin given to food consumed and exercise undertaken. Ideally, the insulin exactly matches the child's energy expenditure and food intake. To achieve this balance, diabetics must frequently check either their urine or blood to ascertain that the level of free sugar in the blood is appropriate. Too little insulin can result in a diabetic coma; too much can produce an insulin reaction (hypoglycemia) that can lead to unconsciousness and seizures. Illness can alter the usual balance, making control especially difficult. Stress also appears to influence metabolic control directly, as well as having an indirect effect through lowering regimen adherence (Hanson, Henggeler, & Burghen, 1987).

Thus the diabetic walks a tightrope: measuring food intake, injecting insulin, matching both of these to energy expenditure, and testing constantly to insure that appropriate levels of sugar result. Watching for signs of hypoglycemia such as headache, irritability, or shakiness and carrying a ready supply of sugar is necessary. Finally, careful checking of the feet for signs of disease is important. Foot care can help to avoid diabetic gangrene, one of the many potential complications of diabetes caused by vascular changes related either to the disease or to insulin injections. Vascular changes can also result in retinopathy, a leading cause of blindness in young people (Skyler & Cahill, 1981). Neuropathy, or changes in the nervous system diminishing sensation and control, is another long-term consequence of uncontrolled diabetes. Thus there are both short- and long-term potential negative consequences for failing to adhere to the diabetic regimen (Jovanovic & Peterson, 1981).

Considering the severity of these consequences, one might expect excellent adherence to the regimen. However, the complicated, difficult, and inconvenient procedures that have to be carried out are sometimes discouraging. Adherence requires a knowledge of the timing of various responses such as glucose testing and insulin injection, belief that adherence is important, skill to correctly perform adherence behaviors, and motivation to follow through. Recent studies suggest that, although knowledge of the regimen is related to better adherence and metabolic control (e.g., La Greca, 1982), knowledge in both parents and diabetic children is often poor (Epstein, Cobrun, Becker, Drash, & Siminerio, 1980; Johnson et al., 1982). Furthermore, knowledge and skill regarding one aspect of the diabetic regimen (e.g., giving injections) does not imply knowledge and skill regarding other tasks (e.g., testing urine or blood; Johnson, 1984). Thus one of the important contributions of the pediatric psychologist to diabetic care is the development of specific and effective regimen education programs (Rapoff & Christophersen, 1982; Varni, 1983).

Planning a diabetes education program involves many factors. Attention to the child's developmental level (La Greca, 1988a) and psychological readiness to learn (Garner & Thompson, 1978) is vital. Other clinicians have emphasized the importance of allowing parents and children to verbalize their fears and misconceptions (Ehrlich, 1974; Koski, 1969). Techniques such as modeling and shaping are also undoubtedly useful. Regular review of what the family has learned is important because, as some researchers have found, errors often increase rather than decrease with experience, probably because initial training is forgotten (Watkins, Roberts, Williams, Martin, & Coyle, 1967).

Another contribution related to education is the pediatric psychologist's assessment of the parents' and children's health beliefs. Even a sound knowledge of the diabetic regimen is unlikely to be implemented unless the individual believes that such adherence will make a positive difference. In fact, some studies show knowledge to be inversely related to metabolic control (e.g., Williams, Martin, Hogan, Watkins, & Ellis, 1967), perhaps because noncompliant patients receive extra education. These efforts nevertheless typically fail to increase the patients' adherence (Johnson, 1984).

Recent studies suggest that diabetes-specific health beliefs are related to both self-reported adherence and physiologically measured metabolic control (Brownlee-Duffeck et al., 1987; La Greca & Hanna, 1983). However, no studies to date have successfully demonstrated the ability to alter diabetic patients' health beliefs and subsequent regimen adherence. This area offers a challenge for future research.

The pediatric psychologist can, however, be instrumental in removing barriers to adherence. La Greca (1988a) suggested that children with few barriers are significantly more adherent to the regimen and in better metabolic control. She cited such barriers as forgetfulness, social situations (fear of being teased or stigmatized for eating snacks or using insulin), scheduling problems, and problem-solving deficits as major stumbling blocks to diabetic adherence. All of these barriers seem amenable to behavioral interventions.

The successful demonstration of improved adherence due to psychological treatment is relatively recent, but the area is growing. Although self-monitoring strategies alone do not seem effective (e.g., Epstein et al., 1981), self-monitoring of blood glucose levels that is rewarded by parental praise and a point system has been used successfully to improve adherence and metabolic control (Carney, Schechter, & Davis, 1983). Similarly, parental monitoring in addition to written instruction and token rewards has improved adherence in foot care, urine glucose testing, and diet (Lowe & Lutzker, 1979).

Some interventions have been successfully automated. Collier and Etzwiler (1971) utilized a teaching machine to administer diabetic education. More recently, Gilbert et al. (1982) utilized a filmed modeling procedure to teach children to self-inject insulin. Such modalities suggest a variety of possibilities. Not surprisingly, the most effective treatments tend to incorporate many components, such as intensive education, involvement of parents, reinforcement, and self-monitoring (e.g., Epstein et al., 1981). Future research by pediatric psychologists and their colleagues may determine the most cost-effective combination of treatment techniques.

Thus far, our discussion has centered on adherence to the diabetic disease regimen. However, regimen adherence is only one factor in good metabolic control. There is increasing evidence that stress influences diabetic management (La Greca, 1988b) and that it may influence metabolic processes directly rather than through its effects on behavioral adherence (Hanson et al., 1987). That is, stress may directly affect the body's use of injected insulin and ingested sugar, rather than (or in addition to) causing the diabetic to be less adherent to the medical regimen. Some treatment agents have focused on increasing the coping skills of young diabetics (Follansbee, La Greca, & Citrin, 1983); such interventions may ultimately influence metabolic control. This seems an important and fascinating area for future research.

There are many other approaches used by pediatric psychologists that cannot be presented in detail in this overview. They include school-based interventions, family therapy, and group therapy. School-based interventions have been discussed in chapter 3. Briefly, these include education of the teacher and classmates to the nature of diabetes; special provision for snacks, urine or blood testing, and insulin injection; and arrangements for any missed work to be made up without extra stress or penalty (for a detailed discussion, see Drotar, Crawford, & Ganofsky, 1984).

Family therapy is often considered an important adjunct treatment for children with diabetes. Minuchin (1974) performed some of the classical work with structural family therapy, demonstrating the negative effects on metabolic control that are seen when a diabetic child becomes the focus of concern in a troubled marital dyad. The difficulties encountered by the child draw attention away from the parents' own marital problems and thus become functional for the family. Therapy involves extricating the child from the marital dyad and dealing directly with interspousal stress. Other researchers have used family-based therapies that focus on communication training and conflict resolution, as well as individual sessions that teach methods of establishing autonomy, identifying anxiety, and utilizing progressive relaxation (Bauer, Harper, & Kenny, 1974). Transactional Analysis, which focuses on the present and on developing new solutions to problems, may also be employed (Haimowitz, 1972). Other methods ask parents to simulate having diabetes and to work with multifamily groups to facilitate perspective sharing (Citrin, Zigo, La Greca, & Skyler, 1982).

Group experiences can go beyond family therapy to normalize the experience of having diabetes. For example, summer camps for diabetic youngsters provide children the opportunity not only to learn better self-care but also to see peers with diabetes engaging in pleasurable and skill-producing recreational activities. In addition, groups can be used to extend clinical interventions. Garner and Thompson (1978) described group therapy for diabetic adolescents in which discussion of methods of coping with vocational opportunities and dating, as well as diabetic management and self-care, provided opportunities for problem solving and for emotional support. Young diabetic adults or older adolescents who have achieved athletic or vocational success can participate as models and can discuss their own coping strategies.

SEIZURE CONTROL

Seizures in children arise from abnormal neurological activity that results in sudden cognitive, sensory, and motor disturbances. Recurrent seizure activity is referred to as *epilepsy* (Bird, 1982). There are a variety of types of seizures, bearing the labels *grand mal, petit mal, absence, Jacksonian, akinetic, focal, myoclonic,* and *psychomotor.* Seizures are categorized in terms of electroencephalograph (EEG) results, anatomical and etiological factors, clinical factors, and frequency (Ellison, Largent, & Bahr, 1981; Gastaut, 1970), as well as by their possible nonorganic bases (Massey & Riley, 1980; Williams, Spiegel, & Mostofsky, 1978).

The major method of seizure control has been through anticonvulsant medications, which can reduce or eliminate seizures in 70 to 80 percent of affected children (Johnston & Freeman, 1981). However, because adherence to anticonvulsant regimens is often very poor (Freiman & Buchanan, 1978), one of the major challenges for the pediatric psychologist is increasing anticonvulsant medication adherence, using techniques similar to those just described for diabetic patients. Even with perfect adherence, however, medication fails to control all seizures and is often accompanied by disagreeable side effects (Gordon, 1978; Reynold, 1978). Thus, when possible, other methods of control should be sought.

There is some evidence that, by using EEG feedback, epileptic patients can learn to control their seizures by increasing the production of sensorimotor rhythm (or SMR, a 12- to 14-Hz sinusoidal waveform over the sensorimotor cortex) or by decreasing slow waves, spike activity, or high voltage EEGs. For example, Finley (1976) decreased seizures in an adolescent epileptic by using biofeedback to teach the patient to increase SMR activity. Similarly, Lubar and Bahler (1976) treated eight epileptics suffering from akinetic, focal, grand mal, myoclonic, and psychomotor types of epilepsy. They taught these patients to increase 12- to 14-Hz EEG activity by giving them visual or auditory feedback when such waveforms were produced and by inhibiting such feedback when 4- to 7-Hz EEG activity, slow wave, or spike activity occurred. Patients who were able to increase 12- to 14-Hz EEG activity demonstrated clinically significant seizure reductions.

Kuhlman (1978) used biofeedback training with five epileptic patients, noting that feedback contingent on the production of 9- to 14-Hz EEG activity resulted in a 60 percent decrease in seizures for three of the patients. However, he found that enhancement of SMR activity of 12 to 14 Hz was not necessary for seizure reduction and argued that the decrease of high amplitude-low frequency waveforms, rather than the production of a given rhythm, resulted in seizure reduction.

This premise was examined by Cott, Pavloski, and Black (1979), who utilized either time-out for slow wave and spike EEG activity, feedback on SMR waveforms, or both. They found the time-out condition to be as successful as the SMR plus time-out treatment. This finding suggests that reducing preseizure slow wave and spike EEG activity, not increasing any specific preseizure waveform activity, is essential to seizure reduction. This exciting research needs to be extended in the future with child patients, and developmentally specific methods of training need to be examined.

There is evidence that seizure control can also be obtained without EEG feedback by utilizing cognitive-behavioral techniques. For example, Ince (1976) treated a 12-year-old boy who suffered from grand mal and petit mal seizures, both of which were uncontrolled by anticonvulsant medication. The boy learned to use relaxation techniques and then received systematic desensitization focused on a hierarchy of anxiety-provoking events such as being teased by peers or having a seizure in public. He was instructed to use his relaxation techniques whenever he had a preseizure aura or was unduly anxious. This treatment resulted in a decrease from 10 grand mal and 25 petit mal seizures per week to no seizures during 6-month follow-up.

Some investigators have successfully used straightforward behavior modification techniques that bear little resemblance to biofeedback or relaxation techniques. For example, Gardner (1967) described a case history in which reinforcing seizure-incompatible behaviors, such as appropriate play, and ignoring seizure occurrence eliminated seizures in a 10-year-old girl. Similarly, Zlutnick, Mayville, and Moffat (1975) utilized a series of behavior modification techniques with five children who had a variety of differing seizure forms, demonstrating successful reduction of seizure frequency in four of the five patients. They treated several of the children by abruptly and vigorously interrupting characteristic preseizure activity. Specifically, the treatment agent was told to shout "No!" at the first sign of preseizure behavior and then to grasp the child sharply by the shoulders and shake him or her once. Such treatment required that the child have a clearly discernible preseizure activity; the only subject who was unsuccessfully treated did not have such identifiable preseizure behavior. For the successfully treated subjects, treatment effects resulting in seizure activity decreases were clearly demonstrated by the use of a reversal design.

Zlutnick et al. (1975) also demonstrated seizure reductions using a DRO (differential reinforcement of other behavior) procedure with a mentally retarded adolescent epileptic. This girl had a chain of behaviors preceding a major motor seizure in which her body became rigid, she clenched her fists and raised her arms straight in front of her, her head snapped back, and she grimaced. During treatment, when the girl raised her arms, the treatment agent lowered her arms to her side, waited 5 seconds, and, when no seizure occurred, praised the girl effusively and rewarded her with a piece of chocolate. This treatment decreased seizures to near zero. Lane and Samples (1984) similarly treated a 3-year-old developmentally delayed girl with severe seizure activity.

One of the exciting aspects of the treatment study described by Zlutnik et al. (1975) is that the authors focused on implementation. The treatments were conducted by parents or schoolteachers, were easy to understand and to replicate, and were clearly effective. Pediatric psychologists wishing to implement such programs bear the responsibility for assessing the problem, programming, training the treatment agent, and carefully evaluating the treatment integrity and effectiveness. However, the likelihood that the program will be continued and treatment gains maintained is greatly enhanced by the use of a change agent who is a part of the natural environment. The following case study, abstracted from Balaschak (1976), describes this principle in the treatment of an 11-year-old epileptic girl:

> At 18 months of age, Joan was diagnosed as having an organically based seizure disorder. This diagnosis was not unexpected; Joan's parent and two siblings also had seizure disorders. Joan grew up with serious problems relating to peers and functioning independently. When she was 9, she began having very unusual, lengthy seizures that were diagnosed as "hysterical"; she began weekly psychotherapy sessions to assist in diminishing these psychogenic seizures.
>
> By age 11, Joan was having several seizures per week. Although she claimed she could not tell when she was about to have a seizure, she was observed to take precautions with breakable objects prior to her seizures. Otherwise, she did not take precautions to guard her physical well-being, such as sitting down so she would not fall.
>
> Beginning in mid-November, Joan was treated by her teacher, who made up a "good times chart" that tallied Joan's seizure-free morning, lunch, and afternoon periods. If Joan received tallies in each time period (total = 15), she received a candy bar. Although the psychologist consultant suggested an easier-to-achieve criterion for reward, Joan wished her goal to be a completely seizure-free week. The teacher also rewarded Joan with praise for appropriate social interactions during this period and showed a film on epilepsy to the class, with questions from peers for Joan to answer after the film. The special token program and praise for social interactions was continued throughout the next 4 months.
>
> Unfortunately, Joan became ill with mononucleosis and could not attend school in March and April. When she returned, her teacher refused to continue Joan's reinforcement program, apparently believing that it would be too stressful for Joan to maintain the program and to make up missed schoolwork too. Despite urging from the consulting psychologist, the teacher refused to cooperate and the program was dropped.
>
> Prior to the program, Joan had seizures on 60 percent of the school days. During the program, her rate dropped to 21 percent. Once the program was discontinued, the rate rose once again to 62 percent.

Thus, regardless of whether the pediatric psychologist focuses on medical adherence, self-control techniques, or operant tactics, the maintenance of the program in the "real world" is likely to depend upon support from the child's significant others, such as teachers and parents. These issues are considered at greater length in the conclusion of this chapter.

MANAGEMENT OF ACUTE AND CHRONIC PAIN

The two categories just described—diabetic regimen adherence and seizure control—both involve attempts to engineer appropriate medication consumption when such medications may be forgotten or avoided. Acute or chronic disease-related pain, however, presents the pediatric psychologist with a different challenge: that of limiting or eliminating the desire for analgesic medication.

There exist an unfortunate number of pediatric disorders that are typically accompanied by acute and/or chronic pain of organic origin. Hemophilia is one such disorder. Most people recognize hemophilia as a hereditary disorder in which blood coagulation is deficient, causing intermittent uncontrolled bleeding. However, not everyone is aware that there are short- and long-term side effects of this unpredictable bleeding. Short-term side effects include excruciating acute pain. Long-term side effects include internal influence on various parts of the body, including the joints. Repeated hemorrhaging into the joints, termed *hemarthroses*, can eventually cause destruction of the cartilage and pathological bone formation that impairs joint mobility. This causes chronic pain similar to that of osteoarthritis. Severe joint pain, immobility, and physical limitations are thus a predictable part of the disease (Steinhausen, 1976). In fact, this chronic, degenerative arthritis is one of the most frequent challenges for physicians treating hemophilia; it influences 75 percent of adolescent and adult hemophilia patients (Dietrich, 1976).

It is important for the pediatric psychologist to recognize that these two types of pain must be regarded very differently. Acute pain functions as a warning of a new bleeding episode. As such, it is likely to be accompanied and amplified by anxiety. Reducing the anxiety and treating the bleeding with intravenous factor-replacement therapy is the immediate task when acute pain is experienced.

The chronic pain component does not have such an adaptive, signalling function; it can result in both dependence on analgesic medication and impaired life functioning (Varni & Gilbert, 1982). Thus, when treating chronic arthritic pain in the child with hemophilia, the pediatric psychologist must devise a system that effectively limits maladaptive responding to chronic joint pain but that does not limit adaptive responding to end the bleeding signaled by acute pain (Varni, 1981a).

A variety of treatment techniques have been attempted, most using cognitive-behavioral strategies such as imagery, deep muscle relaxation, biofeedback, and hypnosis. Lebaw (1970, 1975), for example, employed self-hypnosis in combination with deep muscle relaxation, reporting successful pain reduction as well as reduction in the amount of factor-replacement products needed to effect blood clotting. Similarly, Varni (1981a, 1981b) constructed an intensive intervention employing several components, including techniques created through extrapolation of earlier research with arthritis patients. This work suggested that increased warmth (such as that caused by warm weather, hot showers, or friction massage) decreased pain sensations and increased mobility of the joint (White, 1973). Varni employed progressive muscle relaxation; meditative breathing; imagery involving scenes with warm sand, sun, and colors; and thermal biofeedback. For deep muscle relaxation, Varni outlined 25 steps; these steps specified muscle tension of individual muscle groups, relaxation, and cognitive focus on deep breathing. He then moved on to meditative breathing, in which slow, deep breaths were paired with the word *relax*. The patient was asked to visualize this word on a blackboard in warm colors such as red and orange. Guided imagery focused on increasing blood flow to the affected joint and on the simulated sensation of warmth. Finally, thermal biofeedback was used to give the subject feedback after each trial. This treatment resulted in decreased pain across an 8-month follow-up period and was accompanied by an average increase of 5.6 degrees Fahrenheit over baseline levels of warmth in the afflicted joint.

Varni, Gilbert, and Dietrich (1981) utilized similar techniques for a 9-year-old boy with hemophilia. The child suffered from both chronic arthritic pain and repeated acute pain. His acute pain could not be treated via factor-replacement therapy because at age 4 the boy had developed a factor-replacement inhibitor, an antibody that neutralized the effects of the replacement products. Thus therapy focused on relieving both types of pain. The same multicomponent treatment utilized by Varni (1981a, 1981b) was employed, but the imagery for acute bleeding pain involved pleasant, distracting scenes rather than scenes suggesting warmth. A 1-year follow-up demonstrated a dramatic decrease in the child's pain perception, as well as improvement in mobility, sleep, and general overall functioning. The child also increased his school attendance and decreased the number of hospitalizations. Perhaps most important, his parents reported that he was less depressed and anxious during bleeding episodes because he felt that he now had the skills to influence his perception of pain.

In addition to assisting the hemophilic child in managing both acute and chronic pain, the pediatric psychologist might also assist the child by focusing on adherence to the complex treatment regimen and to necessary therapeutic exercise (Varni, 1983). Improving family functioning can also indirectly help by diminishing stress and anxiety that can contribute to the child's pain. Thus the pediatric psychologist treating the hemophilic child might arrange or conduct family therapy (Handford, Charney, Ackerman, Eyster, & Bixler, 1980) or parent education focused on teaching problem-solving skills and offering support (Saunders & Lamb, 1977). As was noted earlier in chapter 3, involving the parents in factor-replacement therapy at home also reduces stress and avoids disrupting school and peer relations (Strowcynski, Stachewitsch, Morgan-Stern, & Shaw, 1973). Like the contributions to diabetic regimen adherence and seizure control, the treatment of hemophilia-related pain thus requires a holistic approach.

These three medical targets for psychological intervention demonstrate a variety of intervention strategies that have evolved mostly in the last decade. Many of the techniques—such as the behavior modification methods used to increase diabetic regimen adherence, decrease seizures, and eliminate reports of chronic pain—have been borrowed from other areas of psychology. Others, like EEG biofeedback for seizure reduction or home factor-replacement therapy for acute pain related to hemophilia, show a creative combination of cognitive-behavioral methods and medically based technology. All of these examples demonstrate the importance of a holistic approach that transfers as much control to the child and family as possible.

NATURALISTIC COPING STRATEGIES IN ASTHMATICS

This last section will focus on the creation of an educational program designed to teach competent self-management of chronic asthmatic disease processes. We will describe not only the techniques used, but also the method used for developing the educational program.

Asthma is the most common chronic disease of childhood (Davis, 1972). It symptoms can range from annoying wheezing, to difficulty in breathing that ends ongoing educational or recreational activities, to status asthmaticus, which can result in death. Asthma is characterized by frequent school absences and restricted activities with family and peers (Siegel et al., 1982) and can have strong deleterious effects on individual and family functioning (Steinhauer, Mushin, & Rae-Grant, 1974). It resembles several of the disease categories already discussed in terms of the child's often poor adherence to an exercise and medication regimen (Bergner & Bergner, 1976; Dolovich, Hargreave, & Wilson, 1975).

McNabb, Wilson-Pessano, and Jacobs (1986) have described an exciting new methodology for establishing successful treatment techniques to be used with asthmatic children. Rather than beginning with traditional psychological techniques or disease-based medical interventions, McNabb et al. utilized a tool called the *critical incident technique* to assess interventions already being used by asthmatic children and their families. This technique allowed the investigators to construct a list of techniques that had already been effectively used in the natural environment. The investigators were able to enumerate the steps necessary for each technique, systematically evaluate how effective differing techniques were, and assess how frequently children selected each technique for use.

Each respondent was asked to describe either notably effective or ineffective methods of coping with asthma, supplying details relating to such factors as the ongoing situation; the response to the situation; the outcome of the response; reasons the response was effective or ineffective; any persons contributing to the response; and relevant demographic information such as the who, what, when, and where of the situation. In all, 164 children, 161 parents, 91 teachers, 74 nurses, 48 school nurses, and 26 physicians contributed information. These 564 respondents contributed a total of 1,374 incidents, with the average number of incidents described ranging from 1.6 per teacher to 3.0 per physician.

The incidents were then categorized into four general competency areas, including prevention, intervention, compensatory behaviors, and external controlling factors (these last two areas were ultimately combined). *Prevention* encompassed 349 incidents, with eight major categories: (1) avoids allergens, (2) avoids irritants and precipitants (such as temperature extremes or fumes), (3) controls emotions that trigger attacks, (4) takes action when exposed to allergens or irritants to minimize effects, (6) takes preventive medication, (6) ensures access to medication, (7) uses "mind control" to prevent attacks, and (8) cooperates in the treatment of upper respiratory infection.

Intervention involved 763 incidents and included five major categories: (1) takes at least one ameliorative action when attack starts (e.g., drinks fluids, uses postural drainage, decreases activity, uses relaxation); (2) practices a variety of different kinds of intervention strategies, cued to the severity of the symptoms; (3) develops or requests individually adapted intervention; (4) uses medicine correctly; and (5) remains calm during an attack.

Compensatory behaviors were observed in 199 incidents and were grouped into five major positive categories and three negative categories. The positive categories included (1) discusses asthma and necessary restrictions with peers, (2) accepts responsibility for managing own condition, (3) exhibits determination to overcome limitations, (4) accepts regimen even if painful or restrictive, and (5) avoids using asthma to manipulate people or get attention. The negative categories included (1) denies, resents, hides, or blames self for asthma; (2) authority figure hinders treatment (e.g., an adult forces the child to do something to aggravate the asthmatic condition); and (3) family problems trigger child's attack.

McNabb et al. (1986) utilized these naturally occurring competencies to create an individualized education program they called AIR WISE. The children who received this training program demonstrated better control over their asthma, as indicated by fewer emergency room visits, than did a control group not receiving the competency training. This self-management education program is exciting for a variety of reasons. First, it demonstrates an ability to limit the negative effects of this debilitating and life-threatening disorder. Second, it utilizes self-management techniques, as well as supportive assistance from significant others (such as seeking help when needed, accepting reminders from others, etc.). Such behaviors are likely to be maintained in the natural environment. Finally, it demonstrates the viability of using the critical incident technique to program actual intervention strategies. As will be detailed in chapter 7, one of the primary skills the pediatric psychologist can bring to the field of medicine is research expertise. With research tools like the critical incident technique, exciting inroads can be made in developing new psychologically based intervention strategies to combat physical disease.

It seems important to reiterate here several points made throughout this chapter. The first step toward successful change in a child is the discovery of an effective change technique. The second step is the implementation of the technique with that particular child and demonstration that the technique effectively deals with a problem. The third step, at once crucial and often ignored, is to ensure that the technique is consistently applied at appropriate times in the child's day-to-day environment. Doing so often means that the pediatric psychologist must alter not only the child's behavior but also that of parents, teachers, or physicians. Reinforcement programs for compliance are only as effective as the rewards they promise, which must be contingent upon only the requisite behaviors. Relaxation is effective only if performed correctly and consistently. Finally, research on psychological techniques must extend to methods of establishing environmental support.

In addition to contributions in improving children's adjustment to chronic disease, pediatric psychologists can also reduce distress due not to disease but to the medical intervention itself. The following chapter will consider the psychological management of these negative side effects of medical diagnosis and treatment.

Chapter Six

Psychological Interventions to Reduce Medically Caused Distress

With increasingly successful but aggressive diagnostic and therapeutic techniques, current medical treatments may often be accompanied by extensive anxiety and pain. There are many ways of conceptualizing the task of reducing such medically caused distress. For the purposes of this discussion, we have divided the targets of intervention into four groups. First, there are procedures that are not painful but are threatening. Second, there are procedures that are both threatening and painful. In some of these cases, the child must deal with acute pain and anxiety while remaining motionless and cooperative. In others, specifically surgery, the child surgery patient is anesthetized during the active intervention, and treatment focuses on diminishing anxiety prior to anesthesia induction and on dealing with pain after the procedure. Finally, there are certain medical settings that demand special interventions, such as emergency rooms, intensive care suites, and so on. This chapter will describe some of the preventive preparation procedures within each of these four categories and will highlight the different challenges for the child and hence for the pediatric psychologist.

THREATENING PROCEDURES

Cast Removal

During the removal of an orthopedic cast, the child is exposed to a variety of threatening stimuli. Applying a saw to a limb that has been injured is clearly frightening. The noise and vibrations from the saw, the fear of being cut, the burnt smell of the cast as it is destroyed, and the sight of the often wrinkled and grey-looking limb are anxiety-provoking stimuli that can be rendered less frightening through appropriate preparation. Informing children about the sequence of events involved in the procedure is important and should include the information that they must remain very still, that the saw will not touch their skin, and that the limb that has been in the cast will initially appear a bit different from their healthy limb. Using distracting imagery or self-instruction (e.g., "All I have to do is sit still. This will all be over soon. See, my cast is coming off, just as it should.") is also helpful. For very frightened children, deep muscle relaxation and coaching may be necessary.

Procedures like cast removal, in which many unusual but nonpainful sensations are present, seem ideally suited to the use of *sensory information techniques*. One of the first demonstrations of successful preparation for orthopedic cast removal, conducted by Johnson, Kirchoff, and Endress (1975), utilized sensory information. Children from 6 to 11 years of age received either no message; an audiotaped message with general information about the saw, scissors, and typical procedures; or sensory information concerning how the saw might sound and how the limb under the cast might look and feel. This latter group of children exhibited less observable distress during removal of the cast than the other groups and showed lower pulse rates, indicating less anxiety.

Because cast removal is a relatively common procedure, one might expect it to be the subject of frequent research. However, very few studies have empirically examined methods for reducing distress during cast removal.

Anesthesia Induction

Anesthesia induction has also been the subject of very little research, despite the fact that most children find this process very threatening. Although it involves no vibrating saw that can potentially damage tissue, being "put to sleep" can be very frightening to a child, especially if the child is psychologically unprepared. Some physicians have recorded horror stories of "stormy" anesthesia inductions, in which a crying, screaming child is held down and feels he or she is being suffocated with a poisonous gas, resulting in long-term psychological complications such as stuttering or nightmares (Jones, 1985a, 1985b). In addition, lack of cooperation during anesthesia induction can cause medical problems. Crying and pulling away can cause potentially serious respiratory problems and lead to medical complications (Eckenhoff, 1953).

A variety of undocumented "helpful hints" exist in this area. For example, Wilson (1982) suggested that preparation agents wear a Mickey Mouse doll around their necks or on their stethoscopes when they describe the induction procedure to the child on the pediatric ward. Then, when they encounter the child during the actual induction, the child will recognize the familiar Mickey Mouse doll and be more likely to cooperate. Gatch (1982) described a number of useful strategies, including carrying a small child into the operating room rather than using a stretcher and performing induction with the child cradled in an adult's lap rather than lying on his or her back. Some physicians have recommended that the parent assist in anesthesia induction (Mason, 1978), but such a practice is very rare. Training by the pediatric psychologist of selected parents might make such a practice more likely.

One of the best-known empirically validated methods for anesthesia induction was investigated by Vernon and Bailey (1974). They used a film of four child models, a young boy and girl (age 5) and an older boy and girl (ages 8 and 9, respectively). These child models were each seen, one at a time, being wheeled into the operating room, receiving the blood pressure cuff on their arms and stethoscope on their chests, and allowing the anesthesiologist to place the mask over their faces and the nurse to lightly restrain their hands and upper bodies. When the anesthesiologist and nurse stepped back, in each case the child was seen to be peacefully asleep. The film gave a positive but accurate portrayal of a smooth induction. When compared to children who did not see the film, children who viewed the film immediately before their preoperative sedative were rated by observers as being less anxious and more cooperative during entry to the operating room, as anesthesia induction began, and during the first minute of induction.

An adequately prepared child is not only less psychologically and physically distressed but can also assist in anesthesia induction by relaxing, focusing on an image, and even helping to hold the anesthesia mask to his or her face:

Four-year-old Adrianne had been walking on a small retaining wall when she fell sideways onto the cement, breaking her arm just above the wrist. Her parents rushed her to a local children's hospital. An X-ray confirmed the fracture and the need for a general anesthetic so that the bone could be set. The pediatric psychologist assisted in the preparation of the frightened, injured child. He showed her how to lie quietly and to lightly hold the mask full of "sleepy medicine air" with her uninjured hand. Slow, rhythmic breathing was paired with a scene of "a pink rabbit hopping through the meadows." The induction went very smoothly, and the child's first words on awakening were "Where did my rabbit go?"

The pediatric psychologist can be instrumental in supplying procedural and sensory information, in teaching the appropriate responses, and in supplying the knowledge that there is nothing unsafe (the mask will not smother) or painful about the anesthesia induction process.

Perhaps because anesthesia induction and cast removal do not involve pain, pediatric psychologists have not dealt with them clinically nor focused research attention on them as often as other procedures. This would seem an important task for future research, given the threatening nature of both procedures. Reassurance that the child will not experience pain cannot be offered for the medical procedures considered in the next section. Here, a good portion of the anxiety elicited by the procedures is a function of the veridical knowledge that "It's gonna hurt!"

THREATENING AND PAINFUL PROCEDURES

Venipunctures and Injections

Children often report that venipunctures and injections are the most fear-provoking hospital events (Eland & Anderson, 1977; Poster, 1983). They are also among the most frequently occurring medical interventions. Surprisingly, there is currently little consensus concerning the best preparations to use for needle-based medical procedures. Some clinicians have advocated very directive instructions. For example, Hedberg and Schlong (1973) reported that, during mass immunization clinics, children who received stern instructions to "stand on their feet and not be silly" were less likely to vomit or faint than were uninstructed children.

However, most clinicians advocate more sensitive preparation. For example, Fernald and Corry (1981) reported that, when a laboratory technician prepared children for a venipuncture or fingerstick in an empathetic fashion (e.g., "I'll bet the alcohol feels cold. In a moment, I'm going to stick you. You're probably feeling scared . . ."), they cried, winced, and refused to comply less than if they were prepared in a stern manner (e.g., "Act big and brave. Remain very still."). Half of the sternly prepared children were angry and believed the lab technician had tried to hurt them, whereas only 5 percent of the empathetically prepared children reported such emotions and beliefs.

The same cognitive-behavioral techniques used with chronic pain patients have been shown to aid children in coping with injections and venipunctures. For example, vivid mental imagery (Ayer, 1973) and sensory relabeling plus a skin coolant (Eland, 1981) have been shown to aid coping and reduce the report of pain due to injections. Filmed modeling plus a coping technique package of relaxation, self-instruction, and imagery-distraction also have been shown to be successful in increasing cooperation and decreasing observable distress (Peterson & Shigetomi, 1981), often with results that surprised laboratory technicians accustomed to drawing blood from unprepared children:

Our preparation program had only been underway for 2 weeks, and we were naturally a little apprehensive about staff response to it. As I was setting up for the program, a man in whites (a hospital uniform) appeared at the door. "Are you the lady who's working with the kids from peds?"

"Yes?" I swallowed.

"Well, what have you been doing to them?" he demanded.

I began an elaborate rendition of the modeling and coping techniques we were using, but he cut me off. "I've never seen anything like it," he thundered. "The last three kids have come into the lab, helped themselves into the chair, rolled up their sleeves, and offered me their arms. I can't believe it!" With that, he was gone. I breathed again. Was this appreciation at last?

Pediatric psychologists can contribute not only by preparing hospitalized children who must undergo these procedures but also by teaching lab technicians and nurses to administer the methods and proving to them that venipunctures and injections are easier to deliver to a prepared child. Furthermore, because almost all children experience routine injections during childhood, teaching well children methods of coping with injections would be useful.

In contrast, the next procedures to be discussed are relatively uncommon in the general population but are unfortunately frequent for child cancer patients. They not only involve injections but also additional painful interventions with needles.

Lumbar Punctures and Bone Marrow Aspirations

Pediatric oncology patients experience a variety of stressors that demand coping skills. These stressors include nausea, hair loss, weight loss, and disfigurement occurring in the process of their treatment (Adams, 1976; Azarnoff, 1976). Such children tend to be more psychologically isolated and anxious than other chronically ill children, perhaps because of the aversiveness of the procedures they must endure and because the possibility of death is always present (Spinetta, 1977). Thus the regular diagnostic procedures they must endure, often for weeks or months, are especially threatening. The most common diagnostic procedures are lumbar puncture (sometimes called *spinal tap*) and bone marrow aspiration. During a lumbar puncture, children lie on their sides curled into a fetal position, an anesthetic is injected, a needle is inserted into the spinal cord, and spinal fluid is drawn. This procedure usually takes 10 to 15 minutes. In a bone marrow aspiration, children typically lie on their stomachs; after a topical anesthetic is injected, a larger needle is inserted through the exterior of the anterior or posterior iliac crest, and bone marrow is drawn. If the marrow sample is obtained on the first insertion, the procedure takes about 5 minutes.

Both procedures result in varying amounts of acute pain, both require that the child remain motionless, and both create distress that is exacerbated by anxiety (Katz, Kellerman, & Siegel, 1980). Anxiety seems a natural response to such procedures; because the outcome of either procedure can be an indication of either remission or relapse, the significance of the tests is considerable. Even for children too young to understand the threat, the tension in their parents and physicians is likely to contribute to their anxiety. Furthermore, the very nature of the tests, in which the children must lie still and cannot see what is being done and in which adults must often hold them down, adds to the distress.

Because bone marrow aspirations and lumbar punctures are frequently repeated procedures, some unprepared children evolve adaptive strategies of their own. These strategies bear close resemblance to the cognitive-behavioral methods used by pediatric psychologists. Other children have a poor response to the procedures. Their anxiety and tension heighten the pain, their lack of cooperation prolongs the procedure and necessitates physical restraint, and they become increasingly sensitized each time a procedure must be accomplished:

> Marianne and her mother usually arrived looking pale and determined. After the nurse set up the treatment suite but before the physician arrived, Marianne would take off her wig (her hair had fallen out during chemotherapy) and dress, don a hospital

gown, and position herself on the treatment table. Her mother would hold her hand, and together they would create an image of floating on an air mattress on a lake, with warm sun beating down on Marianne's back and cool water beneath her. By the time the physician arrived, Marianne was no longer cognitively in the treatment room. Her face remained smooth and expressionless, save for an occasional brief flicker of discomfort, throughout the procedure. She never moved or cried out. It was hard to believe she was only 8 years old.

Steve, on the other hand, was a 10-year-old boy who had experienced a traumatic first lumbar puncture. A resident had inserted the needle into a nerve, causing sudden and excruciating pain to radiate down Steve's spine and one of his legs. The pain lasted for several days. After that, Steve's mother had great difficulty getting him to the treatment room. Once there, he would delay with requests to use the bathroom, get a drink, change rooms, etc., and when his delay tactics were no longer tolerated, he would become combative. Sedation and half the nursing staff were required to hold Steve down. His cries for help and screaming could be heard throughout the clinic. He emerged from the procedures sobbing, exhausted, and nauseated.

The study of natural coping techniques, as well as the examination of traditional psychological and medical interventions, is important. Not surprisingly, the techniques used most frequently by pediatric psychologists to deal with the distress produced by these diagnostic procedures are similar to those used with pain associated with chronic disease. Hypnosis was one of the earliest techniques described as useful in relieving distress (e.g., Kellerman, Zeltzer, Ellenberg, & Dash, 1983; LaBaw, Holton, Tewell, & Eccles, 1975). It appears particularly appropriate with highly anxious pediatric patients (Zeltzer & LeBaron, 1982). Relaxation and distraction techniques also appear to be successful in lowering both uncooperative behavior and reports of pain, especially when used in combination with behavior therapy techniques such as modeling and reinforcement. In one of the most successful treatment studies to date, Jay, Elliott, Ozolins, and Olson (1983) treated 10 children who had been referred due to extreme distress during lumbar punctures and bone marrow aspirations. They utilized a multimodal treatment involving controlled breathing, positive imagery, reinforcement for lying still and using the breathing exercise, modeling using dolls and medical instruments, and coping self-instruction. For 9 of the 10 children, distress was reduced 40 percent or more over baseline levels, and it remained at a reduced level for 5 of these subjects. One of the strengths of such an intervention is that it allows the child to select the preferred technique or techniques for minimizing distress and thus may tap into a child's natural coping strategies.

Physicians have often bypassed the use of behavioral coping strategies in favor of pharmacological solutions for reducing anxiety and pain. Recently, multicomponent behavioral techniques have been compared with the use of a mild sedative (Valium) in helping child cancer patients cope with diagnostic procedures. Jay, Elliott, Katz, and Siegel (1987) described the use of relaxation training, distraction, and goal setting. The pediatric psychologist coached the child throughout the procedure to relax and to concentrate on positive images. Adaptive responding was rewarded by a small trophy (children mentioned the external reward as an important component of the treatment). Children receiving the behavioral preparation reported lower levels of pain, were observed to be less distressed, and had lower pulse rates than children in the no-treatment control condition. The children who received Valium scored at an intermediate level, nonsignificantly less well than the behaviorally trained children but nonsignificantly better than the control group. It is unclear whether the benefits of both mild sedation and behavioral techniques would be additive, resulting in even more effective coping, or whether the sedation would limit the child's ability to utilize the self-control procedures. The differential utility of each of these individual behavioral techniques in isolation, as well as their combined effect with sedating medication, remains a question for future research. However, in the last 5 years, this field of inquiry has moved from an absence of potential effective treatments to a growing clinical and research focus on diminishing distress in pediatric oncology patients. A similar rapid and recent growth has been seen in the next problem area.

Burn Hydrotherapy

Although significant pain and anxiety are involved in diagnostic oncology procedures, most do not compare with the suffering and fear that occurs secondary to the treatment of serious burns in children.

Nearly half of the 2 million burn injuries that occur each year involve children (Dimick, 1977). In addition to isolation, immobilization, and disfigurement (Clarke, 1980), these children face extreme pain. Concern about compromising the child's respiration and fluid intake necessitates minimal use of analgesics. Past authors reported continuous screaming on a children's burn ward to be a matter of course (Long & Cope, 1961); for current staff, reduction of pain on a burn unit remains a difficult goal.

Perhaps one of the most painful aspects of treatment of the burned child has been briefly described earlier in chapter 4. Hydrotherapy, or *tanking*, which involves placing the burned child in water, and *debridement*, or removing dead tissue by scrubbing it away with sterile gauze, are common treatments for children with serious burns. Children's crying and thrashing often delay the procedure (Varni, Bessman, Russo, & Cataldo, 1980), and some children learn that, if they vomit or defecate in the water, they are quickly removed. All of these uncooperative strategies prolong treatment, exacerbate pain, and increase the risk of infection.

A variety of methods have been reported anecdotally in the past to help reduce distress in burned children. These include hypnosis (Bernstein, 1965; Wakeman & Kaplan, 1978), self-instruction and meditation (Weinstein, 1976), and play therapy (Levinson & Ousterhout, 1980). Recently, Elliott and Olson (1983) provided an empirically validated demonstration of reductions in pain and increases in cooperation during hydrotherapy with four pediatric burn victims. They utilized relaxation and deep-breathing techniques, attention distraction, and tangible rewards. In addition, they employed emotive imagery with some of the children; in this process, the children were taught to imagine a scene in which they were asked to endure the treatment as a heroic act for a favorite storybook hero. These techniques greatly reduced pain and escape-related behavior, but only when the pediatric psychologist was present to coach the child in the use of the techniques.

Kelley, Jarvie, Middlebrook, McNeer, and Drabman (1984) also used a multicomponent behavioral treatment for two children receiving hydrotherapy treatment. Television cartoon viewing was used as a distracting stimulus, and the children were rewarded with star tokens for inhibiting distress behaviors such as crying. Both of the children's pain-related behaviors, such as crying or groaning, declined during treatment and increased following the end of treatment. The authors stressed that their desire was not to reward suppression of complaints but to offer the children alternative behaviors and reward the use of these alternative strategies. They pointed out that modeling and coping techniques have been proven effective with child surgical patients and should also be effective in assisting burn patients, additionally urging that future research be conducted on these methods for reducing distress in pediatric burn victims.

The past several sections have considered preparation for medical procedures ranging in intensity from cast removals, to venipunctures, to burn treatments. Very few investigations exist for any of these areas; however, more research efforts have been directed toward preparation for surgery, to be described next.

Preparation for Surgery

The earliest and most frequently researched programs for preparing children for medical procedures focused on child surgery patients. There are probably more empirical studies dealing with that population than for any other we have considered so far. Because most child surgery protocols involve a variety of threatening and potentially painful procedures (e.g., venipuncture for bloodwork prior to surgery, preoperative injection of a sedative, anesthesia induction, and postoperative pain), it is not surprising that pediatric psychologists have focused on this potentially stressful ordeal.

The early literature on pediatric patients' response to surgery noted that it was commonplace to misinform children about an intended surgery; thus a child who had expected to go shopping or to the circus would arrive instead at the hospital to have an operation (Chapman, Loeb, & Gibbons, 1956). Separation from the family was also a matter of course, with resultant distress (Prugh, Staub, Sands, Kirschbaum, & Lenihan, 1953) and potential for long-term emotional problems (Douglas, 1975). (See chapter 3 for discussion of the need to focus on family processes.) The first improvements seen in preparing a child for surgery were increased sensitivity to issues of trust and reassurance that the parent would not have to leave (e.g., Brain & Maclay, 1968).

These changes were followed by increasing agreement that the child should receive accurate information about the coming medical procedures (Prugh & Jordan, 1975). The majority of professionals in pediatric medicine now give at least lip service to the value of preparation. However, we should note that, even with current research support and technology, not everyone in the field of medicine believes that children should be told anything about the medical procedures they will undergo. Recently, a nurse in charge of children's services at a major hospital remarked, "I don't care what the 'studies' say; it only worries a child to be told about a procedure. You are better off just showing up, gently restraining the child, and getting the job done." We anticipate that children at this hospital become very vigilant, never knowing when someone will "just show up" and do their "job." Currently, though, the modal response is at least to acknowledge the child's right to be informed.

There are many early descriptions by practitioners concerning how information is best given to children. The use of play therapy techniques to describe what will happen in terms of procedures and sensory detail (Abbott, Hansen, & Lewis, 1970) was one of the first techniques to be clinically validated (Cassell, 1965). It is likely that Cassell's (1965) "puppet therapy" actually involved modeling and procedural information in addition to dramatic play. The more dynamic use of play therapy to work out misconceptions about surgery; to allow "retaliatory play," in which the child is urged to respond aggressively toward medical personnel (e.g., Chan, 1980); and to promote the use of art or play to explore surgically related fears (e.g., Crowl, 1980) remain unevaluated but frequently used techniques that may or may not reduce distress.

Similarly, the use of books to prepare children for medical procedures has been suggested. Altshuler (1974), Crocker (1979), and Roberts (1986) reviewed books that attempt to inform children about hospital procedures and described their apparent clinical characteristics. However, bibliotherapy for pediatric surgery patients has not been evaluated, and thus the real merits of this method also remain unexplored.

There are three major treatment technologies that have been explored by pediatric psychologists and empirically shown to be successful in reducing distress in child surgery patients. These include *stress point preparation*, *modeling preparation*, and *coping and stress inoculation*. Because they have been experimentally validated, they should be regarded as preferred techniques.

Stress Point Preparation

Wolfer and Visintainer (1975) described a procedure in which the child and parent received individualized communication from a nurse at critical points of stress during hospitalization. Such stress points were defined as occurring on admission to the hospital, before the blood test, preceding the first night's stay, prior to the preoperative medication and the trip to the operating room, and immediately following return from the recovery room. At these various points, the nurse prepared the child by using a doll as a model and telling a developmentally appropriate story about what would happen. Mothers received information, reassurance, and the opportunity to ask questions and express their concerns.

Within families who received this special care, parents were less anxious and more satisfied with the nursing care, and children were observed by an independent rater to show fewer distress behaviors at all of the identified stress points. The treated children responded more adaptively before and after surgery, exhibiting less resistance to anesthesia induction and greater fluid intake and earlier voiding after surgery.

Other investigators have also reported improved child behavior and decreased parental anxiety as a result of individualized interventions by the treatment nurse (e.g., Ferguson, 1979; Skipper & Leonard, 1968; Skipper, Leonard, & Rhymes, 1968). However, such interventions are very intensive in terms of time and labor and thus may not be available to all hospitals. The use of a single preparation program prior to hospitalization has also shown positive results, with less cost.

Modeling Preparation

Melamed and her colleagues have produced the largest data set demonstrating the effectiveness of using a film of a child model to relieve distress in child patients. In an early study, Melamed and Siegel (1975) showed half of their subjects the film *Ethan Has an Operation*. This 7-minute film portrays a boy who is admitted to a children's hospital; who undergoes a blood test, presurgical injection, IV insertion, and anesthesia induction; and who recovers from the surgery, first in the recovery room and then on the pediatric ward. The child demonstrates adaptive behavioral reactions to all of these procedures, and his voice narrates the story, indicating adaptive emotional responses as well. Children who viewed the film reported fewer hospital-related fears and demonstrated less anxious and distressed behavior than did children who did not view the film. Subsequent studies, many of which are summarized by Melamed and Siegel (1980), replicated the positive effects of this program.

Pinto and Hollandsworth (in press) also demonstrated the value of a filmed child model. They utilized a single film with either a child or a father narrating the film. Children viewed the film either alone or with a parent. The film covered 13 scenes, ranging from admission, X-ray, orientation to the pediatric ward, encounters with medical equipment, interactions with nurses and doctors, blood tests, transportation to the operating room, awakening in the recovery room, and follow-up postoperative exam. Parents who viewed the film had lower physiologically measured and self-reported anxiety than did parents not viewing the film. Interestingly, parents who did not view the film but whose child did were less anxious as assessed by physiological measures and self-report than parents who did not view the film themselves and whose child also did not view the film. Children who viewed the film had, in comparison to children who did not, a more positive response to every dependent variable measured.

The use of a film can be far less expensive and less labor intensive than the earlier described stress point preparation. However, most films portray one specific hospital setting and routine. If a unique film must be created for every hospital setting, the cost effectiveness of the film is greatly decreased. Peterson, Schultheis, Ridley-Johnson, Miller, and Tracy (1984) compared Melamed and Siegel's (1975) *Ethan Has an Opera-*

tion, which was filmed and initially evaluated at a children's hospital in Ohio, to a locally produced videotape entitled *Nathan Has an Operation*, which had a similar script but was taped at the same location in which the children viewing the film would undergo surgery. The researchers contrasted both films with the use of a program involving a puppet model (a teddy bear rather than an actual child), who again followed a similar script but who used three-dimensional equipment and narration rather than actual dialogue. They found that all three modeling techniques resulted in fewer maladaptive behaviors and lower rates of parental anxiety than were seen in children who did not view a program but who received attention from the pediatric psychologist. None of the modeling techniques was superior to the others. This finding suggests that a hospital with equipment available but not much staff time can elect to use either a local or commercial film, and a hospital without equipment or equipment funds but with skilled staff available can use a puppet model, at least with elective minor surgery patients like those in the Peterson et al. study.

Attention to such details by the pediatric psychologist researcher may go far toward creating preparation techniques that will actually be used in the field. Coping skills training, the final method to be discussed, has also been subjected to such questions of cost-effectiveness by comparing it to already existing forms of preparation.

Coping and Stress Inoculation

Peterson and Shigetomi (1981) attempted a component analysis of modeling and coping skills training with four groups of elective child surgery patients. Each group viewed a film of a puppet model describing local hospital procedures and practices. In addition, one group viewed the film *Ethan Has an Operation* and one group received coping skills training similar to the techniques used with chronic pain and invasive diagnostic procedures (reviewed in chapter 5 and earlier in this chapter). Specifically, children and their parents received training in cue-controlled relaxation involving the meditation word *calm*, deep breathing and deep muscle relaxation, self-instruction, and the use of distracting positive imagery. Parents were designated as their children's therapists. They were asked to rehearse the methods with their children and to coach them in the use of these coping methods while in the hospital. A final group of children viewed the puppet show film and received coping skills instruction.

The coping skills instruction was especially useful in decreasing children's maladaptive responding and increasing cooperation in invasive situations such as the venipuncture blood test and the preoperative injection. Children receiving both the modeling treatments and the coping skills training performed most adaptively in response to these procedures. Children receiving the coping skills training also seemed to eat more foods, drink more liquids, and void sooner than the other children, and their parents reported less anxiety and greater feelings of competence. This study suggests that coping skills are a useful addition above and beyond the effects of procedural information, puppet modeling, and filmed child modeling.

Would the children in this experiment have fared as well without receiving modeling in addition to the coping skills preparation? It is difficult to say, but an experiment by Zastowny, Kirschenbaum, and Meng (1986) suggested that coping skills training can be useful even in the absence of a model. These authors presented parents with a 16-minute film on the nature of stress, training in deep breathing, methods of distraction, and stress inoculation techniques (i.e., preparation, confrontation, coping with feelings, and self-reinforcement). Children whose parents received such training were more cooperative, especially during threatening procedures such as the preoperative injection, and were rated as better adjusted following surgery. The parents receiving the training also reported less anxiety.

Because psychological preparation for surgery has been recognized as an important charge for pediatric psychologists for well over a decade, a variety of treatment methods have been validated as successful tools, and research in this area is increasing. In contrast, there have been no studies and very few anecdotal reports of methods of dealing with children in special medical locations such as emergency rooms, intensive care units, and isolation suites. Because such locations impose their own special stresses on child patients and are an important challenge for pediatric psychologists, these situations will be briefly considered next.

THREATENING LOCATIONS

Emergency Rooms

Peterson and Mori (1988) argued that, in terms of psychological preparation and support, perhaps the most underserved and underresearched medical population is pediatric emergency admissions. For children under the age of 5, 85 percent of hospitalizations are emergency admissions, and visits to the emergency room (ER) appear to be increasing for children of all ages (United States Department of Health, Education, and Welfare, 1978). Typical ER activity epitomizes the concept of stress. Medical personnel are often hurried and terse; their concerns are physical rather than psychosocial. Victims in various stages of suffering and bleeding are readily apparent, and family members who are shocked, grieving, or hostile line the waiting area. Because it may be some time before a problem receives medical attention, tempers are often short. For a child who is already injured, the anxiety of the parents coupled with the ER atmosphere and a long wait can intensify fears and discomforts.

There are two ways in which pediatric psychologists can approach this problem. Because visits to the ER are almost always an emergency rather than elective treatment, the individual child cannot be prepared for that visit in advance. However, some pediatric psychologists have advocated preparing healthy children in the school classroom for the possibility of emergency intervention. Roberts, Wurtele, Boone, Ginther, and Elkins (1981) demonstrated that a slide and audiotape presentation describing common hospital procedures lowered the self-reported anxiety and hospital-related fears of elementary school children. Similarly, Peterson and Ridley-Johnson (1983) demonstrated that a didactic lecture illustrated with actual medical equipment was as effective as the commercial modeling film *Ethan Has an Operation* and that both successfully reduced medical fears in fourth- and fifth-grade children. Interestingly, even the control group decreased in fearfulness (although the treated groups decreased significantly more), probably because even children in the control group experienced repeated exposure to medical equipment in the assessment process. The preparation of well children to undergo medical procedures, including simple exposure to demystify medical equipment, is one way in which the fears associated with ER admissions could be reduced.

A second method is to have a preparation agent present in the ER to work with the children as they come in. Alcock, Berthiaume, and Clark (1984) described such a program. They began by paying attention to the ecology of the emergency room. Chairs were clustered together to promote supportive communication, indirect lighting was used to reduce visual stress, and child-relevant art and objects such as mobiles and kites were used. There were even pictures placed on the ceiling for viewing by children on stretchers. A child-life worker was assigned, first to ensure the physical comfort of the child patient and family, and second to reduce stress by listening, offering information, and engineering play during the waiting period (which can be as long as 2 hours). A booklet containing information and the story of a peer model was available as well.

Alcock et al. (1984) do not have empirical data concerning the success of these strategies, but past work with children experiencing stressful medical procedures suggests that stress point support (Wolfer & Visintainer, 1975), information (Prugh & Jordan, 1975), instructive play

(Cassell, 1965), and peer modeling procedures (Melamed & Siegel, 1975) are all effective techniques worthy of investigation. Pediatric psychologists working in the ER or in intensive care units will need to consider methods of explaining, relabeling, or distracting children from fear-provoking sights and sounds involving other patients, as well as techniques for dealing with the children's own fear and distress.

Intensive Care Units

As noted above, the intensive care unit (ICU) shares with the ER a stressful, hurried medical atmosphere and the presence of other patients whose suffering often provokes fear. Furthermore, children are more likely to be separated from their parents in an ICU than on a regular pediatric ward (Prugh & Jordan, 1975). The ICU is also more crowded and contains more threatening medical equipment than an ordinary ward (Rothstein, 1980).

There have been very few studies involving children in ICUs and no sound empirical studies we know of that demonstrate systematic reductions in stress or anxiety in pediatric ICU patients. The assessment studies that do exist suggest that, contrary to the common belief that children are not fully conscious and block out external events, they are often very alert to ICU phenomena (Barnes, 1975), although they may distort much of what they see and hear due to high fear arousal. Cataldo, Bessman, Parker, Pearson, and Rogers (1979) found that children in ICUs emitted a high rate of stereotypic behavior and spent much time staring into space. When they were given the opportunity to play with a toy or to interact with a child-life worker, their rate of attention, engagement, and positive affect greatly increased, and stereotypic behavior declined.

Pediatric ICUs are also stressful to parents. Miles and Carter (1982) have categorized this stress into eight dimensions, including (1) sights and sounds of the ICU, (2) the child's appearance, (3) treatment procedures, (4) the child's behavior, (5) the child's emotions, (6) staff communication, (7) staff behavior, and (8) parental rule deprivation. They further suggest a need to develop intervention strategies aimed at reducing these stressors.

The effectiveness of frequent psychological consultations in the ICU setting to dispel misconceptions, provide alternative adaptive behavior, and teach coping skills has not been empirically demonstrated, but past research strongly suggests the utility of providing accurate information

(Prugh & Jordan, 1975), supplying opportunity for instructive play (Cassell, 1965), and teaching coping skills (Peterson & Shigetomi, 1981). Future clinical intervention and research in this area is badly needed.

Isolation

Rather than facing extensive activity, crowding, and fear-provoking reactions of other patients, the child in isolation must cope with loneliness, feelings of abandonment, boredom, and sensory deprivation. However, like children in other special medical locations, these children can also benefit from the services of the pediatric psychologist.

Children with compromised immune functioning must be protected even from the normal viruses and bacteria that are a part of everyday life. *Reverse isolation* is the term used to describe preventive methods to ensure that such children do not contract any disease until they are able to recover. In reverse isolation, the child is placed in a special room. Visits are strictly limited, and visitors must wear special gowns and medical masks over their mouths and noses. The children themselves wear gowns that come from sealed packages. If they are allowed to eat, rather than receive nutrients by IV, their food is specially screened and prepared.

Loneliness and boredom set in rather quickly. Separation from family members and the absence of a normal daily routine create special stresses. As is the case for pediatric ICU patients, stereotypic behavior and lack of cooperation are common in children in isolation suites. Symptoms appear that are similar to those reported in early sensory deprivation experiments, including insomnia and hypersensitivity. Preliminary study has indicated that ignoring inappropriate responding and systematically reinforcing adaptive responding is helpful for adult isolation patients (Redd, 1980). Children who receive multimodal treatment, with regular visiting and play activities, appear to show no long-term negative effects of isolation, but it is unclear how they would fare if such a comprehensive program were not provided (Kellerman, Rigler, & Siegel, 1979).

Although the empirical validation of intervention methods for children in isolation has not included suitable controls, it seems likely that methods of increasing interpersonal contact and giving meaningful stimulation would be beneficial. Mail and telephone communication where possible should be valuable (O'Meara, McAuliffe, Motherway, & Dunleavy, 1983). The creation of an audiotaped family message (McCain,

1982), or even contact with peers, siblings, and parents through closed-circuit television, could also be arranged. For the child who is well enough, school lessons and computerized games could relieve boredom. Again, this is an area ripe for clinical intervention and research exploration.

Throughout our discussion of methods of intervention, we are forced to acknowledge that clinical practice of a technique has, of necessity, preceded empirical demonstration of the value of that practice. This imbalance leads us to our final chapter in this book, which considers the future challenges to pediatric psychology. First among these challenges is the establishment of a sound research base for future practice in the field.

Chapter Seven

To the Future

The contributions of pediatric psychologists in the future will rest on decisions being made in the field today. The establishment of a sound research base for clinical practice, with particular focus on the most effective behavioral techniques currently in use, is imperative to the development of the field of pediatric psychology. Uniform training criteria and a focus on prevention as well as remediation of childhood disorders are also crucial. In this closing chapter we sample, rather than comprehensively review, findings in each of these areas to illustrate the major issues currently being considered in the field. Although there are other important issues for the future, these seem essential to the continued fulfillment of the promise of pediatric psychology.

ESTABLISHING A RESEARCH BASE

We began this book by noting that pediatric psychology is a young field, only about 2 decades old. In this short time, the field has matured from a state of "childhood" to growing independence and responsibility. The development from "adolescence"—the field's present self-conscious self-evaluation and identity seeking—to full maturity will be hastened by the generation of a solid research foundation. Currently, clinical practice in pediatric psychology has of necessity outstripped its research underpinnings. However, the last decade has seen a real coming of age in research sophistication within the field; there is every indication that, in the next decades, these research capabilities will come in line with clinical capabilities and even begin to lead rather than follow clinical practice.

There are a wide variety of reasons why the generation of a research base is a vital development within pediatric psychology. First, research abilities are one of the strengths the pediatric psychologist can bring to the "marriage" with the pediatric physician. Although medical training is placing more emphasis on research, there is far less training in research methodology and statistics within medicine than within psychology (Friedman & Phillips, 1981). The ability to operationalize a problem, to quantify results, and to discern real from chance findings is essential to most of the problems in pediatric medicine today.

Later in this chapter, we will discuss training of the pediatric psychologist in more detail, but it is commonly accepted that a sound research background is required (Davidson, 1988; Tuma, 1982b). The application of scientifically validated therapeutic techniques is the essence of the Boulder model, in which a clinician is expected to be both a practitioner, actively rendering clinical services, and a scientist, actively interpreting and contributing to the scientific literature. To be welcomed in pediatric medicine as a colleague will require skills not only equivalent but complementary to those of the pediatric physician. Furthermore, the oversupply of pediatricians expected in the future may result in pediatric psychologists who do not have complementary skills being replaced by physicians (Maher, 1983).

Why is the empirical validation of clinical techniques so vital? A quick look at medical history will answer this question. For many years, physicians bled their already debilitated patients in the belief that doing so would somehow draw off illness. Initially, physicians scorned Louis Pasteur (a nonphysician) and his foolish notion that bacteria caused death in women following childbirth. They refused to wash their hands after seeing each patient, as if to do so would be to admit culpability for past illnesses and deaths. Many more recent examples document well-meaning but harmful interventions within psychology as well. For example, there are still some ill-informed clinicians who suggest the use of catharsis activities (verbally or motorically acting out strong emotions like anger) for children, even though such activities have clearly been shown to elicit rather than decrease such negative reactions as aggression (Mallick & McCandless, 1966). It would seem fairly clear that, in most cases, data and appropriate analysis provide better service to children than does clinical intuition.

Even if a given therapist were one of those remarkable few who could discern the direct effects of a given intervention in the absence of data, most problems faced by the pediatric psychologist are more complex than whether intervention *A* has effect *B*. As noted in our discussion of the consultant relationship in chapter 2, the reductionistic style of problem solving characteristic of medical training is much more effective in discerning main effects than complex interactions. This orientation leads many physicians to ignore more complicated psychosocial data. As Paul noted in 1967, the question posed to the psychologist is rarely "Which treatment is effective?" but rather "Which treatment applied by which person in which setting for which client at which time will have which outcome?" The challenges in pediatric psychology most often appear as interactions among characteristic child variables, demographic and family variables, developmental level and disease stage, and a host of other contributing features. Only the most carefully conceived empirical exploration can hope to begin to describe the myriad of influences that determine treatment outcome.

Research can not only assess the positive aspects of an intervention but, if carefully designed, can describe negative outcomes as well. Traditionally based techniques may be refined through research, and new interventions can be discovered. The study of naturally occurring coping strategies, similar to the critical incident techniques described earlier in the context of asthma treatment, may make particularly effective contributions. Evolving new and previously unapplied treatment techniques is one of the most exciting aspects of research in pediatric psychology.

The pediatric psychologist who, over the course of a year, relieves suffering in 50 children through the use of a novel technique has made an important contribution. The pediatric psychologist who can *prove* that his or her method relieved suffering in 50 children has the chance to inform other practitioners and thus help thousands of children, making an incalculable contribution. It is vitally important to be able to pass helping skills on to other professionals, and the mentor system is too limited and too slow to do this effectively.

It is also essential to be able to persuade individuals who make funding decisions in medical settings that the pediatric psychologist supplies an important and useful service and to prove to practicing pediatric psychologists that new methods can enhance their clinical skills. One of the most important tools the pediatric psychologist has for effecting implementation of psychological techniques is research that attends to considerations of cost-effectiveness, compares relevant interventions, and demonstrates that treatment goals can be obtained (Peterson &

Mori, 1988). Research alone will not result in implementation (Stolz, 1984); political power, personal contacts, persuasiveness, and knowledge of the medical system are required as well (Peterson & Mori, 1987). However, in the absence of research demonstrating the efficacy of psychological interventions, the other components involved in implementation decisions are of little value.

Finally, establishing a research program can help the pediatric psychologist find a personal identity and prevent the burn-out that can come from repeated service delivery (Drotar, Benjamin, Chwast, Litt, & Vajner, 1982). Through research, one maintains contacts with individuals throughout the country having similar skills and interests. The sense of making a more lasting contribution and of gaining greater understanding of one's area of expertise is especially important.

What areas within pediatric psychology currently require a more extensive research base? A simplistic but nonetheless realistic answer might be "All areas." Throughout this book, we have repeatedly called for improved and more extensive research. Examining differing methods of managing the consultant relationship and replacing personal opinion of what strategies are valuable with empirical data are enormously challenging and important areas. Additional research on the special aspects of the child population is also badly needed. For example, improving current knowledge of children's developmentally specific understanding of illness might enhance the pediatric psychologist's ability to obtain an accurate symptom history from a child. Research on dealing effectively with the parents and siblings of an acutely ill child, an injured child, or a child with a chronic illness is essential to effective family-based therapy. There is also very little research on intervening with peer systems and the school system.

Our chapters dealing with differing disorders within pediatric psychology (see chapters 4, 5, and 6) also repeatedly called for additional research. Such research might focus on limiting the physical and emotional effort in the treatment of nonorganic enuresis, identifying the critical aspects to be considered in the placement of a mentally retarded child, documenting an effective treatment for chronic abdominal pain, demonstrating a systematic ability to determine when an infant with nonorganic failure to thrive or an abused child would be better removed from the home, describing the critical elements in diabetes regimen adherence at different ages, and outlining the components of effective preparation for a painful medical procedure with a very young child who has had a previous negative experience and who is "denying" the current surgery. We simply know too little in many of these areas to be certain that we are intervening effectively.

An Example: Coping Strategies in Presurgical Preparation

To illustrate the need for additional research and what such research could accomplish, we will examine the last question cited above: "What are the necessary components for effective preparation for a very young child who has had a previous negative experience and who is denying the current surgery?" This question is particularly useful because it is directed toward an area that has been the subject of methodologically sound research for a decade and in which effective interventions are already recognized. Thus it might be assumed that further research is not essential for clinical practice to proceed. It is also (not coincidentally) an area in which we have conducted research and have particularly strong feelings about what is needed.

A casual knowledge of this research area might lead a clinician to assume that preparation for such children should involve a filmed model (the most frequently researched technique in the psychological literature, one repeatedly shown to be successful). However, very few modeling studies have focused on young children. The average age of children in the 14 presurgical preparation studies reviewed by Peterson and Brownlee-Duffeck (1984) was around 7 years. Modeling thus may or may not be the treatment of choice for a young child.

What is known about effective preparation for young children? Undocumented claims from the early medical literature are still held by many to be valid today; these include the notions that preschool-age children cannot understand explanations and must be sedated (Karp & Teuscher, 1947) and that it takes longer and is more difficult to prepare a preschool-age child than an older child (Gabriel, 1977). The empirical literature does support the idea that younger children show more fear and maladaptive responding than do older children (Peterson, Schultheis, Ridley-Johnson, Miller, & Tracy, 1984). This is especially true when the negative reactions are severe (Gabriel & Danilowicz, 1978) or maintained after hospitalization (Harvey, 1980). Preschool-age children recall less preparation information (Melamed, Robbins, & Fernandez, 1982); have a lower level of cognitive development, which makes it more difficult for them to understand medical information (Simeonsson, Buckley, & Monson, 1979); and are less likely to seek out information (Pidgeon, 1981). These factors may place them at special risk.

The bottom line in this discussion is that, although children between ages 4 and 5 tend to be the age group most frequently admitted to United States hospitals (Azarnoff & Woody, 1981), such children have rarely been involved in preparation research. Instead, most studies have focused on older children, who are likely to show larger experimental effects, better understand preparation material, and give more accurate self-report data. The young child seems to be simultaneously more at risk and more underserved than the older child (Goslin, 1978). In a nutshell, we do not really know which preparation is best suited to a young child. Some data with preschool dental patients suggest that sensory information or coping skills preparations may be effective (Siegel & Peterson, 1980, 1981), but this finding remains to be replicated with surgery patients.

To return to our original question, we further complicate the situation by noting that the hypothetical child in question has had a previous negative experience. In the past, investigators conducting methodologically sound research have recognized the difficulty of matching subjects on previous experience and have typically dealt with the problem by utilizing surgically naive subjects. Thus the bulk of this literature does not apply to the experienced child. The few studies that have attempted to assess the impact of prior experience have reported that modeling preparations were ineffective with child dental patients (Ginther & Roberts, 1982; Klorman, Hilpert, Michael, LaGana, & Sveen, 1980) and surgical patients (Melamed & Siegel, 1980) if the children had experienced a previous procedure. Melamed, Dearborn, and Hermecz (1983) concluded that modeling films are particularly contraindicated for young, experienced patients. This may be the case because a modeling film showing only a child responding adaptively to the surgery situation may present information redundant to or conflicting with the experience of such non-naive children. Johnston and Salazar (1979) wisely concluded that it may be necessary to "detoxify" the influence of previous experience before offering preparation for the next experience. Again, some evidence exists that experienced child dental patients can profit from being offered new methods of coping such as training in relaxation and imagery (Nocella & Kaplan, 1982), but this finding remains to be validated with child surgery patients.

We also note that the hypothetical child in question is currently denying the present surgery by acting as if no operation is going to take place. One of the most controversial issues in the area of presurgical preparation today is the extent to which individuals' characteristic methods of coping with stress may interact with the type of preparation they receive. Because past research has yielded conflicting results, this is a very difficult question to answer. This lack of consensus is not surprising, given that researchers have utilized differing preparation methods with differing medical procedures and have measured differing variables. Most of these studies have focused on the extent to which the patient seeks out and is receptive to information (these individuals have been labeled *sensitizers* or *vigilants*) or denies and avoids information (these individuals have been labeled *deniers* or *repressors*). Studies with adults have reported that sensitizers are unaffected (e.g., Andrew, 1970) or helped (Delong, 1971) by information. The controversy regarding adults has concerned the impact of preparation on repressors. Some studies have found that repressing individuals have a negative reaction to preparation in terms of physiological (but not self-report or behavioral) measures (Shipley, Butt, & Horwitz, 1979; Shipley, Butt, Horwitz, & Farbry, 1978). Others have argued that repressors as well as sensitizers benefit from preparation but do so in different ways (Wilson, 1981) or that repressors may benefit from preparation that is complementary rather than congruent to their typical style of denial (Hitchcock, 1982).

The adult literature is confusing enough to cause pediatric practitioners to throw up their hands and retreat to the medical dictum "First, do no harm" by not offering such preparation at all to their child patients. If one extrapolates from the adult literature, the concern that a denying or repressing child could be negatively sensitized through inappropriate preparation techniques seems logical. Such concern may explain, in part, the cancellation of many preparation programs begun in the 1970s (Azarnoff, 1982). However, the few studies described below, which have attempted to identify a characteristic coping style in children, universally concluded that children who seek out information respond more adaptively to hospitalization and surgery than do children who deny such experiences (Peterson, in press). Unfortunately, these studies have offered preparation to all the children in the study and thus do not clearly show whether children who do not seek out information would be better left unprepared or prepared more carefully to give them even more information.

Siegel (1981) noted that children who showed low anxiety, high cooperation, and high tolerance for physical discomfort tended to seek out more information than did children who coped less well. LaMontagne (1984) suggested that actively coping children had a more internal locus of control and argued that the coping style was responsible for the sense of control these children felt. Similarly, Burstein and Meichenbaum (1979) noted that children who selected hospital-relevant toys to play with prior to hospitalization had lower self-reported anxiety following surgery than did children who selected other kinds of toys. Using Rorschach performances and structured interviews, Knight et al. (1979) classified children as coping through intellectualization, denial, displacement, or projection. Children coping through intellectualization had lower levels of urine cortisol (thought to reflect physiological response to stress) than did children coping through denial, displacement, or projection. Melamed (1982) found that physiologically acti-vated children (thought to be like sensitizing adults in their alert respon-siveness to information) recalled more information from a modeling film and were less anxious about hospitalization. Peterson and Toler (1986) used a structured interview to label children's tendencies to seek out information and validated those tendencies through observation of actual medical events. Children who were high information-seekers responded more adaptively both before and after surgery. Finally, Lambert (1984) reviewed several case studies and concluded that coping styles varied from active to passive to resistant. Actively coping children seemed to have an advantage.

The clearest conclusion from these studies is that children who appraise medical stresses by actively dealing with the situation (i.e., ask-ing questions, selecting medically relevant toys, intellectualizing, watch-ing a modeling film, or advocating information seeking) experience less distress than do children who react to appraisal by denying (i.e., not asking questions, selecting nonmedically relevant toys, denying or using displacement/projection, ignoring the modeling film, or advocating remaining still and not actively seeking information). However, the direc-tion of the relationship remains unclear. Perhaps an actively coping child both seeks information and performs well. Alternatively, perhaps it is the information that these children acquire that allows them to avoid dis-tress. As can be seen, the decision of how to prepare the child in our hypothetical example is far from clear-cut.

To further complicate the issue, we should also note that the ideal time to prepare the child, the ideal preparation agent, and the prepara-tion techniques best suited to any given medical procedure are also far from clear. The large majority of studies in the area of presurgical prepa-ration suggest that preprocedure intervention is valuable, but the pediat-ric psychologist of the future will benefit from much additional research on this topic.

There is a kind of "Stygian stables" aspect to this type of discussion, which can be either extremely exciting (i.e., "There are so many interest-ing and important questions yet to be answered!") or very discouraging (i.e., "After 2 decades, we have evolved more questions than we have answered; look how much there is left to do."). We hope future clinical and research practitioners have the former reaction. To avoid discour-agement, we will need to select future avenues to pursue carefully. One of the most promising areas in pediatric psychology today is the applica-tion of behavioral assessment and intervention techniques. We will there-fore turn next to a brief consideration of the potential contributions of behavior therapy to pediatric psychology.

BEHAVIORAL CONTRIBUTIONS

Behavioral techniques have only received widespread use in the last 2 decades, and it seems no coincidence that the rapid development of pediatric psychology has also occurred during that time. Although some early work in pediatric psychology was characterized either by a dynamic orientation similar to that utilized by child psychiatrists or by a strongly psychometric orientation that emphasized the use of tests and pencil-and-paper measurements, pediatric psychology practice has been increasingly characterized by the use of behavioral methods.

Many different reasons exist for the successful application of behavioral techniques in pediatric psychology. First, while minimizing overlap, behavioral techniques complement the skills possessed by most pediatricians and child psychiatrists. Although there is a movement within pediatric medicine toward the use of behavioral approaches, it is clear that such training within medicine is meant to contribute to the pediatrician's generalist skills and that the pediatric psychologist is still likely to be viewed as the specialist in this area (Davidson, 1988). Furthermore, behavioral techniques are firmly grounded in the research tradition familiar to psychologists and thus satisfy the need to establish and operate from the sound research base just discussed.

Finally, and most importantly, behavioral techniques show a striking degree of success in meeting the current challenges in the field of pediatric psychology. The discussion of common disorders targeted for intervention within pediatric psychology (see chapters 4 through 6) focused primarily on behavioral interventions, and there are many other applications in the literature. Consider, for example, the simple behavioral intervention on the effects of reinforcement. The flexibility of this single procedure has been demonstrated in the treatment of nearly every acute and chronic disorder we have discussed. Reinforcement has been shown to decrease chronic pain (Ramsden, Friedman, & Williamson, 1983), increase standing and walking in a child with spina bifida (Manella & Varni, 1981), improve a child's ability to take oral medication (Blount, Dahlquist, Baer, & Wuori, 1984), increase diabetic regimen adherence (Lowe & Lutzker, 1979), maintain hemodialysis patients' special diets (Magrab & Papadopoulou, 1977), decrease fecal soiling (Roberts, Ottinger, & Hannemann, 1977), increase cooperation in the treatment of burned children (Kelley, Jarvie, Middlebrook, McNeer, & Drabman, 1984), eliminate pica in children with lead poisoning (Madden, Russo, & Cataldo, 1980), instill mobility and independent self-care in a child recovering from severe burns (Varni, Bessman, Russo, & Cataldo, 1980), and eradicate trichotillomania (chronic hair pulling) in a child who had been bald for several years due to the disorder (Gray, 1979).

A second example, noted in chapters 5 and 6, involves behavior therapy techniques such as imagery and progressive muscle relaxation. These procedures have been used in a variety of cases involving prevention of pain (e.g., Peterson & Shigetomi, 1981), treatment of acute pain (e.g., Jay, Elliott, Ozolins, & Caldwell, 1983), and treatment of chronic pain (e.g., Varni & Gilbert, 1982). In addition, relaxation treatments have been used to assist in physical therapy exercises in a cerebral palsy patient (La Greca & Ottinger, 1979), to decrease anxiety during asthmatic attacks (Feldman, 1976), and to treat insomnia (Anderson, 1979).

Biofeedback has also been applied in situations other than the chronic pain cases already cited (e.g., Labbé & Williamson, 1983). Specifically, this technique has diminished fecal incontinence in a child suffering from spina bifida (Whitehead, Parker, Masek, Cataldo, & Freeman, 1981) and has improved speech and motor skills in cerebral palsy patients (Finley, Niman, Standley, & Wansley, 1977).

Our discussions have focused primarily on treatment interventions, but it is equally true that behavioral assessment methods are an important part of current practice in pediatric psychology. Eyberg (1985) entitled her presidential address to the Society of Pediatric Psychology "Behavioral Assessment: Advancing Methodology in Pediatric Psychology." She outlined three major areas of behavioral assessment having important application to pediatric psychology. These areas include behavioral interviews, such as the Child Assessment Schedule (Hodges, Kline, Fitch, McKnew, & Cytryn, 1981); behavior rating scales, such as the Child Behavior Checklist (Achenbach, 1978); and direct observational measures.

The use of direct observation is one of the most innovative and important behavioral contributions to the arsenal of the pediatric psychologist. The Dyadic Parent-Child Interaction Coding System (Eyberg, 1974), for example, was designed specifically for use in pediatric settings. It affords the pediatric psychologist a structured method for assessing interactional patterns within problematic families (e.g., families including diabetic children with repeated ketoacidosis from poor regimen compliance, suspected victims of child abuse, or overprotected cystic fibrosis patients). Similarly, Bush, Melamed, Sheras, and Greenbaum's (1986) measure for assessing parent-child interactions during stressful waiting periods prior to medical procedures and Katz, Kellerman, and Siegel's (1980) and Jay, Ozolins, Elliott, and Caldwell's (1983) respective methods of coding behavioral reactions to invasive medical procedures demonstrate sound and very specific strategies for assessing children's distress. Additional methods of quantifying behaviors relevant to children's disease and treatment are likely to evolve in the future.

One of the strengths of the behavioral approach is its apparent simplicity. Reinforcement, for example, is one such versatile and easily understood procedure. However, knowledgeable practitioners are already cautioning against the careless use of behavioral techniques (Davidson, 1988). Roberts (1986) warned against *mind set*, the automatic use of a behavioral technique without complete analysis of the given case. He cited the successful use of time-out in treating psychogenic stomach pain and noted a second case of chronic abdominal pain that might also have been reflexively treated with a similar time-out procedure. However, in the second case, the child's father had died of stomach cancer 2 years previously, yielding a very different set of treatment needs.

The casual application of behavioral techniques without careful assessment, consideration, and monitoring is likely to be ineffective or even harmful. For example, a young cystic fibrosis patient whose noncompliance diverts parents from their marital troubles or a child burn victim who perceives rewards for cooperation as coercive may be unresponsive to apparently sound token-reward programs. Likewise, systematic desensitization appears to be inappropriate for very young children (Ollendick, 1979), and, although self-monitoring can be an effective component in treating some problems (e.g., chronic pain; Varni, 1983), it can be ineffective in treating others (e.g., diabetes; La Greca & Hanna, 1983). Thus specifics such as family history, developmental stage, and disease category must be taken into account when planning any therapeutic intervention, including "simple" behavioral strategies.

The movement toward behavioral pediatrics within medical schools and residency programs is very encouraging. However, one of the gravest risks of such training is that physicians will use behavioral techniques in a cavalier or inappropriate fashion. Davidson (1988) noted that it is very important for physicians receiving limited behavioral training also to receive instruction regarding when to refer more complex cases to an expert. This sort of discussion implies that the pediatric psychologist will have such expertise. We should therefore probably add that particular skill to the criteria described earlier (see chapters 1 and 2): The pediatric psychologist should have health psychology training; should be prepared to operate within the consultant relationship; should have a sound developmental background and a knowledge of family and peer systems; and should have the broad, research-based clinical skills described throughout this book. The bulk of such skills will likely be drawn from behavioral theory.

This description of the pediatric psychologist highlights the many differing educational and experiential components that are viewed as necessities. As such, it opens the way for the next issue of future concern: the training of pediatric psychologists.

PROFESSIONAL TRAINING

In a discipline only 2 decades old, it is not surprising to find that a good deal of controversy and difference of opinion continues with regard to what constitutes adequate training and how one should go about getting it. Early pediatric psychologists received what might be euphemistically termed *post-doctoral, on-the-job training*. Said another way, individuals typically received generic clinical psychology training, often with a specialty in clinical child psychology, and learned to work with children in medical settings through trial and error.

Next, some predoctoral training was begun in the 1960s at selected locations such as the University of Iowa (Routh, 1969) and the University of Oklahoma. Although these programs did not offer a degree specifically in pediatric psychology, they offered the developmental and clinical backgrounds necessary for such work (Routh, 1977). Surveys conducted over the last 15 years show a steady increase in training opportunities (Routh, 1970, 1972; Tuma, 1977, 1980; Tuma & Grabert, 1983). In 1972, Routh reported that 32 out of 100 medical schools surveyed offered some practica training to psychology students. Increasingly, coursework is being joined by practica training in actual medical settings (e.g., Ottinger & Roberts, 1980). Predoctoral internships offering an intensive, full-time training experience in pediatric psychology have been formed. Tuma (1987) reported that there are currently 123 predoctoral internships, 21 postdoctoral internships, and 34 postdoctoral fellowships in clinical child and pediatric psychology.

Although some of the postdoctoral fellowships may be discontinued (Faust, Ulissi, & Thurber, 1980), there is evidence of growth in other training areas. The current oversupply of psychologists in the job market (Maher, 1983) is accompanied by an undersupply of psychologists trained to meet the needs of children and adolescents (VandenBos, Stapp, & Kilburg, 1981). Given the current enthusiasm for health psychology (Matarazzo, 1980), this situation may be particularly true in the health areas. Thus it is essential that a generally accepted set of training guidelines for pediatric psychologists be formulated to meet the current need. There are still a variety of ways in which pediatric psychologists receive their specialization training (Tuma, 1982b). Optimally, specialty material would be presented beginning in the first year in graduate school and would continue through coursework, practica, research apprenticeships, and clerkships, as well as through full-time internships.

Although the need for comprehensive training in pediatric psychology is clear, the necessary components of such training and the sequence in which the components should be delivered is still being debated. Tuma (1982b) described the content of the pediatric psychologist's training as generic psychological training and subsequent specialization in clinical psychology, health psychology, and child psychology. Roberts (1982) outlined four existing models of doctoral-level training: general, adult-based clinical programs allowing specialization in clinical child psychology; clinical child psychology programs; clinical child psychology training within developmental psychology programs; and combined clinical child/school psychology programs. Davidson (1988) traced three primary pathways pediatric psychologists could take after basic core training. These included clinical child, health, and general clinical psychology.

An Ideal Training Model

These descriptions represent a composite of what training should consist of and what is currently available. If we were asked to specify ideal training within pediatric psychology, the layers would involve the following components: (1) a solid grounding in basic psychological processes; (2) training as a clinical child psychologist, including behavioral skills; and (3) training in family therapy and developmental and health psychology, including a specific focus on pediatric psychology.

Generic Training in Psychology

Why provide training in this order? First, most psychologists agree that generic training in psychology is necessary to the pediatric psychologist (e.g., Roberts, 1979; Tuma, 1980). This training typically refers to coursework in various areas of psychology, such as experimental (cognition, learning, physiology), social (group processes, personality), and developmental, as well as statistics and research methods. We have already belabored the point that the pediatric psychologist must have a thorough background in developmental psychology and research. Although the typical didactic coursework in developmental psychology is relevant to the pediatric psychologist, research methodology courses that have not been systematically updated in the last decade are likely to be less pertinent. Many such courses were designed for experimental or social psychology students; tight experimental control, unlimited numbers of subjects, and analogue research are often assumed. Applied or pragmatic research is often regarded as inferior to more "basic" research, and an analysis of variance paradigm is allowed to dictate experimental design.

Pediatric psychologists require the same basic experimental design coursework as other students. However, they also need advanced coursework in dealing with field research problems such as nonrandom assignment of subjects to groups, preexisting subject differences, low numbers of subjects, and multimodal measurement. Increased use of quasi-experimental design and of time series analysis, multiple regression, path analysis, and log linear analysis will be seen in the next decade, and pediatric psychologists must be prepared to use these methods.

Pediatric psychologists have, in the past, accrued the bulk of their research training through mentorship or collaborating with colleagues. Because the pediatric psychologist after internship is likely to be professionally isolated and to be regarded as the mentor for others who have not had research training, it is incumbent upon training programs to ensure that research and design skills are present at the time the degree is awarded.

Field of Specialization:
Clinical Child Psychology

In addition to generic psychological training, a specialization field is necessary. Although there is some disagreement (e.g., Tefft & Simeonsson, 1979), the consensus is that the specialization should be within clinical psychology (Drotar, 1977; Stabler & Whitt, 1980; Tuma, 1975, 1982b). This choice of specialization suggests not only didactic but also practicum experience with child assessment and child intervention, as well as a basic affiliation with practicing clinical psychologists. The history of the Society of Pediatric Psychology, including its early establishment as a subsection of Division 12 (Clinical Psychology) of the American Psychological Association (APA), reflects this consensus. Because the content of coursework and practice within clinical psychology is growing increasingly complex, focusing specialization upon work with children seems wise. Although such a focus should not exclude typical clinical work with adults, clinical work with adults and extensive training in developmental psychology would not adequately prepare the pediatric psychologist. Clinical interventions for children are rarely addressed completely by traditional developmental material, and they differ greatly from the intervention methods used with adults. Thus specialization in clinical child psychology seems requisite.

Further Specialization:
Health and Developmental Psychology

Next, additional specialization in health psychology and in developmental psychology seems essential. A knowledge of behavioral medicine processes and techniques, including "the language and culture of the health care institutions" (Tuma, 1982b, p. 330) and the common psychosocial determinants of the etiology, course, and outcome of illness are important prerequisites to the practice of pediatric psychology. In addition, basic developmental processes, especially those involving cognition and physical development, form cornerstones for the practice of pediatric psychology and are sometimes not covered in clinical child psychology curricula.

Why not suggest that generic psychology training be followed by identification as a health psychologist and specialization in clinical child psychology instead of the reverse: identification in clinical child psychology and specialization in the health area? The intermingling of clinical child psychology and pediatric psychology is stronger historically (Tuma, 1975; Wright, 1967), and some groups currently recognize pediatric psychology as a subspecialty of clinical child psychology (Task Force on Training for Division of Child, Youth, and Family Services, 1983). Actually, this issue is bound to continue to be strongly debated in the future. The APA's Division 38 (Health Psychology) recommends the former structure, viewing the area of life cycle health psychology as a subspecialty of health psychology rather than as a separate field or a part of developmental or clinical child psychology (Task Group on Life Cycle Health Psychology, 1983). As the content necessary to the practice of pediatric psychology becomes increasingly clear, it may be that distinguishing between area of primary identification and specialization will become merely a matter of semantics. That outcome is likely to be optimal because it would suggest that sufficient training in all areas—including clinical child, health, and developmental psychology—existed. Mesibov (1984) cogently argued in his presidential address to the Society of Pediatric Psychology that "the visibility, acceptance, and impact of any group is directly related to its training programs" (p. 9). The current absence of clearly specified training components is a major threat to the integrity of the field. We hope this problem will be erased in the next decade.

Maher (1983), in a discussion of the training of health psychologists, pointed out the need for good basic training because the specific content of some psychological assessment or intervention techniques could be rendered obsolete in the future. We believe one such basic area likely to be valuable in the future is the prevention of health-related disorders. This area has been underresearched in the past, and training in the application of preventive interventions is currently inadequate. Thus we will close this chapter on issues for the future with a brief discussion of the importance of prevention in pediatric psychology.

PREVENTION: THE INTERVENTION OF THE FUTURE

The concept of prevention is not new to pediatrics. In contrast to most of medicine, which is strongly oriented toward the remediation of existing problems, for the last half-century pediatrics has been increasingly involved in the prevention of life-threatening infections and nutritional diseases (Green & Hoelkelman, 1982). The 1970s brought increased focus on psychosocial and lifestyle factors that influence physical well-being, and techniques such as anticipatory guidance and developmental screening were increasingly used within pediatrics (Davidson, 1988; Roberts, 1986).

Anticipatory guidance refers to the pediatrician's anticipating common problems and providing preventive advice and information prior to the parent's actually encountering a problem (Brazelton, 1975). Preventive advice to parents of newborns has typically been directed toward eating and sleeping habits, proceeding later to methods of avoiding injury through "child-proofing" the home and through the use of car safety restraints. As one example of anticipatory guidance, the American Academy of Pediatrics recommends that, during well-child visits, the pediatrician use The Injury Prevention Program (TIPP), a safety survey that allows the physician to ask safety-relevant questions and automatically flags dangerous responses as requiring intervention.

Some pediatricians argue that psychosocial interventions should also take place during regularly scheduled well-child visits as part of anticipatory guidance. Whitt and Casey (1982), for example, asked physicians to engage mothers in brief discussions of relevant tactics for interaction during their infants' 2-week to 6-month health care appointments. This intervention increased mothers' sensitivity to and skilled interaction with their infants through pediatric consultation regarding infant social behaviors.

With this characteristic emphasis on preventing both injuries and interactional difficulties, pediatrics has a history of positive regard for prevention. However, in acute medical care settings, in private practice offices (which average nearly 30 patient visits per physician each day), and in much time-pressured internship and residency training, emphasis is still likely to be on providing immediate care. It is not uncommon for the pediatric psychologist engaged in preventive activities to be challenged by a pediatric physician: "Why are you working with that family when we have sick kids to care for?" (Drotar et al., 1984, p. 254). Physicians are likely to be impressed by medically based preventive solutions, such as immunizations against childhood diseases, or environmentally based tactics, such as placing child-proof caps on medicines, but they are less likely to have enthusiasm for more psychosocial interventions.

The future of prevention in pediatric medicine can thus be strongly influenced by the pediatric psychologist. It is fortunate, then, that research on prevention of disorders in children is very often accomplished by pediatric psychologists (e.g., see the work of authors contributing to Roberts & Peterson, 1984b). Because the determinants of most physical disorders and psychological dysfunctions are based in childhood, it is logical to target a pediatric population to prevent these problems.

If we reconsider treatment targets for pediatric psychologists, it is clear that, within each of the areas described earlier in this volume, preventive clinical practice is needed and research is being conducted to meet that need. Many psychological problems coincidentally occurring in a medical setting are amenable to early efforts. For example, school phobia following illness can be prevented if the challenges are reintroduced gradually, if appropriate reinforcers are presented for school attendance but not for illness behavior, and if social factors (preparation of teachers and peers) are considered. Many "hand-on-the-door" questions on parenting skills and discipline can be dealt with through preventive parent training.

Under the classification of psychologically caused medical problems, we have already noted that some researchers advocate the use of preventive relaxation training with children of adult migraine headache patients (e.g., Hoelscher & Lichstein, 1984). Because of similar links in family history, preventive interventions with the children of parents presenting with chronic abdominal pain or eating disorders such as anorexia nervosa or bulimia would seem important.

Psychologists are just beginning to attempt to prevent psychosocially caused medical problems like child abuse by ensuring that mothers of premature infants spend time early in the lives of their newborns interacting effectively (Klein & Stern, 1971; Widmayer & Field, 1980). Similarly, methods ranging from parent training at the high school level and public education to child drop-off centers have been suggested to prevent abuse (Rosenberg & Reppucci, 1985).

In the area of psychological management of medical problems, poor adherence to treatment regimens may be prevented rather than remediated by appropriate early education and motivation systems, and asthma attacks may be prevented by early use of medication, relaxation, and behavioral coping strategies (such as removing allergens). In addition, our review of psychological interventions to reduce medically caused distress focused primarily on preventive preparations based on the belief that appropriate early intervention can avoid much pain and distress.

Two additional areas of common preventive intervention have been the subject of research in recent years: health promotion and injury prevention. Both are directly related to pediatric medicine and thus will be considered briefly here.

Health Promotion

Health promotion refers to interventions that safeguard health by promoting the avoidance of harmful substances such as too much dietary sugar, salt, and saturated fats, and by increasing health-enhancing behaviors such as the general consumption of high-fiber foods and extra calcium for women. Many experts believe that improvements in morbidity and mortality rates in the future will take place not because of biologically based medical advances but because of changes in lifestyle habits (e.g., Matarazzo, 1980). Because most risk factors that apply to adults also apply to children (Schoenberger, 1982) and because many dangerous lifestyle habits begin in childhood (Albino, 1984), it seems especially important to target children with health promotion efforts.

Cigarette Smoking

An important and well-recognized target for prevention is cigarette smoking. Smoking has been cited as the lifestyle factor contributing most to death and disease in this country (United States Public Health Service, 1979b). Most early antismoking interventions conducted from 1960 to the mid-1970s focused on educating youth about smoking. Such programs resulted in increased knowledge about health and smoking but did not decrease actual smoking (Thompson, 1978). Recent programs have successfully used techniques such as social skills training (Evans et al., 1978), anxiety reduction (Botvin & Eng, 1980, 1982), and a public commitment not to smoke (Hurd et al., 1980). These techniques have documented some short-term success in reducing the number of adolescents who begin smoking and in assisting some adolescents who are smoking to quit. Smoking prevention, as well as prevention of the use of smokeless tobacco, is likely to remain a very important area for future intervention.

Obesity

Another area in which maladaptive habits have been recently challenged is weight control with children. Because at least a third of obese children become obese adults (Lloyd & Wolff, 1980) and because of the long-term cardiovascular risks associated with obesity, this seems an important target for preventive efforts. However, there is potential risk to growth and development in children if dieting is too severe (Mallick, 1983). In addition, the danger of developing anorexia nervosa or bulimia in late childhood or early adolescence exists (Pinkerton, Hughes, & Wenrich, 1982). Careful planning of such programs is therefore desirable.

Some of the more successful programs for adolescents have involved multimodal interventions including self-observation and goals for caloric intake; plans concerning when, where, what, and how to eat; self-instruction; social behavior taught through role play; and financial deposits earned back through weight loss (Coates, Jeffrey, Slinkard, Killen, & Danaher, 1982). Other programs have relied on family-based interventions for both child and parent weight loss (Epstein, Wing, Steranchak, Dickson, & Michelson, 1980) or on school-based interventions (Epstein, Masek, & Marshall, 1978).

Programs focusing on decreasing obesity often include increasing exercise as a goal. Obese children are far less active than nonobese children (Waxman & Stunkard, 1980). Even in individuals of normal weight, aerobic exercise improves the cardiovascular system, reducing high blood pressure and the potential for heart disease (Voller & Strong, 1981). School-based programs that enhance physical fitness are one vehicle shown to be effective (Brownell & Kaye, 1982). Other investigators have successfully applied behavior modification to increase children's aerobic activity levels (Allen & Iwata, 1980).

Dental Hygiene

Another example of a health-enhancing behavior worthy of increasing in children is dental hygiene. The average individual in this country has 15 dental cavities by young adulthood (Albino, 1984), and over a third of individuals over the age of 45 have lost all of their teeth to gum disease (United States Public Health Service, 1979a). The ideal time to acquire appropriate prophylactic habits is early in childhood (Albino, 1984). Preventive programs aimed at young children have shown the value of using instruction plus reinforcement for plaque removal (Martens, Frazier, Hirt, Meskin, & Proshek, 1973), with brushing being monitored by camp leaders (Lattal, 1969) or parents (Albino, Juliano, & Slakter, 1977; Claerhout & Lutzker, 1981). Swain, Allard, and Holborn (1982) described the value of team rewards in "The Good Toothbrushing Game." More cognitively oriented methods have been utilized with junior high school students. For example, Albino (1978) used a contrast between admired personal characteristics and own dental hygiene to improve junior high school students' brushing and flossing. Evans, Rozelle, Lasater, Dembroski, and Allen (1968, 1970) reported that very threatening educational procedures were most effective in improving subjects' *reports* of dental hygiene behaviors. However, more positive educational messages about the social benefits of dental hygiene coupled with detailed instructions were most effective in actually reducing plaque scores.

These different dental hygiene interventions, used with various populations of children, illustrate developmentally appropriate methods. Optimal impact on dental hygiene behaviors would likely be a product of continued programming from preschool to adolescence, with continuity of the differing developmentally specific approaches.

Although there are immediate negative consequences for behaviors such as smoking and obesity and immediate positive consequences for behaviors such as exercising and dental hygiene, the health impact of all of these behaviors is primarily found in adulthood. In other words, for much of health promotion, the real danger of maladaptive responding is not to the child but to the adult the child will become. This is not the case, however, with our final topic for preventive intervention. Preventing injuries is a topic with special importance in the childhood years.

Injury Prevention

We use the term *injuries* rather than the more commonly used term *accidents* because the latter term connotes a random process rather than a series of preventable interactions between actors and environments. Injuries kill more children each year than heart disease, than cancer, or than infectious disease. In fact, injuries take more lives in childhood than the next six causes of death combined (Derschewitz & Williamson, 1977). With one in every three children sustaining a serious injury each year (Starfield, 1977), several million children each year miss school because of injury (Matheny, 1988). Haddon (1984) referred to injuries as the "last of the great plagues to be the subject of scientific inquiry" (p. xxvii).

Although an extensive literature retrospectively describes the etiologies of childhood injuries, attempts to actively prevent injuries in children are more recent. Peterson and Mori (1985) suggested a conceptual model for preventing injuries in which an intervention could have one of three targets: the environment, the caretaker, or the child. The typical intervention methods would be either legislated/mandated or educational/persuasive and would be introduced according to a population-wide, milestone, or high-risk group tactic. The most effective interventions have been legislated environmental changes made population-wide (e.g., child-proof medicine closures; Walton, 1982) or directed toward high-risk groups (e.g., window guards that reduce children's falls in urban areas; Spiegel & Lindaman, 1977).

A large variety of children's injuries cannot be effectively prevented with environmental interventions, even though this method is most effective when possible. Legislated methods targeted toward the caretaker have had some impact, although less than environmental methods (e.g., car safety-seats for children that have reduced the number of child injuries in certain states; Roberts, Elkins, & Royal, 1984). Educational methods directed toward population-wide alteration of environmental factors have been successful in some cases (e.g., Black and Decker Manufacturing has voluntarily installed a safety feature on irons that causes the iron to turn itself off when not in use).

Educational methods applied at a population-wide level to the caregiver have always had a great deal of intuitive appeal. However, most such methods have been quite unsuccessful in altering the use of children's safety restraints (Pless, 1978), decreasing burns (Mackay & Rothman, 1982), and removing home safety hazards (Colver, Hutchinson, & Judson, 1982). These failures have caused some professionals to advocate only the use of environmental interventions, to the exclusion of interventions focused on altering behavior (e.g., Rivara & Barber, 1985; Robertson, 1983). Such a recommendation seems somewhat shortsighted, given recent success in altering caregiver behaviors in removing safety hazards from the home (Tertinger, Greene, & Lutzker 1984) and in teaching children to use seat belts (Roberts & Funurik, 1986), cross streets safely (Yeaton & Bailey, 1978), avoid potential child molesters (Poche, Brouwer, & Swearingen, 1981), and effectively escape from house fires (Jones, Kazdin, & Haney, 1981). Peterson and her colleagues have demonstrated that undergraduate volunteers (Peterson, 1984a, 1984b) and parents (Peterson, Mori, Selby, & Rosen, 1988) can teach children a broad spectrum of home safety skills. Although the bulk of these studies have utilized a relatively small number of subjects, their results are very promising.

It is not possible to do justice to the rapidly expanding area of injury prevention here, but this discussion should give the reader an appreciation of the myriad injury problems still requiring solutions. Many scientists now argue that the area will be best served by a detailed, prospective understanding of the sources of children's injuries (Garling & Valsinger, 1986; Peterson, Farmer, & Mori, 1987). Such research will necessitate familiarity with the developmental proclivities of the child, the systems in which the child resides, and behavioral conceptualizations of intervention strategies. This topic is perhaps a fitting ending to the present discussion because it illustrates one of many future research paths that seem uniquely suited to the field of pediatric psychology.

Epilogue

Pediatric psychology as we have portrayed it most appropriately belongs to the future, not to the past and present contexts we have described. When attempting to characterize the future of such a rapidly developing area, it is difficult not to err on one side or the other—either portraying the field in an overly cautious, even pessimistic fashion (e.g., too little research support exists for our techniques, pediatric psychologists remain unrecognized in the majority of general hospitals, etc.) or in an incautious, exaggerated fashion (e.g., inroads are being made by pediatric psychologists in every disease category relevant to children today, and the field will be a panacea for many forms of distress in the future). We have, of course, tried to steer a middle-of-the-road course, but we should acknowledge that our own bias is typically cautious (but sometimes incautious) optimism. We must also note that, although we have focused this brief text on the role of the pediatric psychologist, the field and the child patients involved are likely to benefit most from an interdisciplinary approach involving many specialists in pediatric medicine.

There are over 20 times more individuals currently specializing in pediatric medicine than in pediatric psychology, and the field still has many battles to win in the areas of training credentials and recognition as a necessary part of the medical team rather than as a luxury found only in select university medical centers. Still, like other pediatric psychologists (e.g., Varni & Wallander, 1984), we can foresee a time when every ill or injured child will receive holistic care from a unified force of medical specialists, including pediatricians, nurses, child-life workers, social workers, and pediatric psychologists. Focus on the child's developing cognitive, social, and affective needs as well as physical condition will be routine, and the child's long-term welfare will be the goal for intervention.

Is such a view realistic? Not without continued work in clinical practice and research, as well as political efforts. And is such a view adaptive? We believe it is. It keeps us and many of our colleagues invested in attempting to actualize this future for the field. We hope this description will attract others to consider a career in pediatric psychology.

References

Abbott, N. C., Hansen, P., & Lewis, K. (1970). Dress rehearsal for the hospital. *American Journal of Nursing, 70,* 23-60.

Achenbach, T. M. (1978). The child behavior profile: I. Boys aged 6-11. *Journal of Consulting and Clinical Psychology, 46,* 478-488.

Achenbach, T. M. (1982). *Developmental psychopathology.* New York: Wiley.

Adams, M. (1976). A hospital play program: Helping children with serious illness. *American Journal of Orthopsychiatry, 46,* 416-424.

Ainsworth, M. D. S., Blehar, M. C., Waters, E., & Wall, S. (1978). *Patterns of attachment: A psychological study of the strange situation.* Hillsdale, NJ: Erlbaum.

Albino, J. E. (1978). Evaluation of three approaches to changing dental hygiene behaviors. *Journal of Preventive Dentistry, 5,* 4-10.

Albino, J. E. (1984). Prevention by acquiring health-enhancing habits. In M. C. Roberts & L. Peterson (Eds.), *Prevention of problems in childhood: Psychological research and applications* (pp. 200-231). New York: Wiley.

Albino, J. E., Juliano, D. B., & Slakter, M. J. (1977). Effects of an instructional-motivational program on plaque and gingivitis in adolescents. *Journal of Public Health Dentistry, 5,* 4-10.

Alcock, D., Berthiaume, S., & Clark, A. (1984). Child life intervention in the emergency department. *Journal of the Association for the Care of Children's Health, 12,* 130-136.

Allen, L. D., & Iwata, B. A. (1980). Reinforcing exercise maintenance using existing high-rate activities. *Behavior Modification, 4,* 337-354.

Altemeier, W. A., Vietze, P. M., Sherrod, K. B., Sandler, H. M., Falsey, S., & O'Connor, S. (1979). Prediction of child maltreatment during pregnancy. *Journal of the American Academy of Child Psychiatry, 18,* 205-218.

Altshuler, A. (1974). *Books that help children deal with a hospital experience* (DHEW Publication No. HSA 74-5402). Washington, DC: United States Government Printing Office.

American Psychiatric Association. (1988). *Diagnostic and statistical manual of mental disorders* (rev. 4th ed.). Washington, DC: Author.

Anderson, D. R. (1979). Treatment of insomnia in a 13-year-old boy by relaxation training and reduction of parental attention. *Journal of Behavior Therapy and Experimental Psychiatry, 10,* 137-146.

Andrasik, F., Blanchard, E. B., Arena, J. E., Teders, S. J., Teevan, R. C., & Rodichok, L. E. (1982). Psychological functioning in headache sufferers. *Psychosomatic Medicine, 44,* 171-182.

Andrew, J. M. (1970). Recovery from surgery, with and without preparatory instruction for three coping styles. *Journal of Personality and Social Psychology, 15,* 227-233.

Asken, M. J. (1979). Medical psychology: Toward a definition, clarification, and organization. *Professional Psychology, 10,* 66-73.

Ayer, W. A. (1973). Use of visual imagery in needle phobic children. *Journal of Dentistry for Children, 28,* 41-43.

Azarnoff, P. (1976). The care of children in hospitals: An overview. *Journal of Pediatric Psychology, 1,* 5-6.

Azarnoff, P. (1982). Hospital tours for school children ended. *Pediatric Mental Health, 1*(4), 2.

Azarnoff, P., & Woody, P. D. (1981). Preparation of children for hospitalization in acute care hospitals in the United States. *Pediatrics, 68,* 361-368.

Azrin, N. H., Sneed, T. J., & Foxx, R. M. (1974). Dry-bed training: Rapid elimination of childhood enuresis. *Behaviour Research and Therapy, 12,* 147-156.

Balaschak, B. A. (1976). Teacher-implemented behavior modification in a case of organically based epilepsy. *Journal of Consulting and Clinical Psychology, 44,* 218-223.

Bandura, A. (1969). *Principles of behavior modification.* New York: Holt, Rinehart, & Winston.

Barnes, C. M. (1975). Levels of consciousness indicated by responses of children to phenomena in the intensive care unit. *Maternal-Child Nursing Journal, 4,* 215-285.

Barowsky, E. I. (1978). Young children's perceptions and reactions to hospitalization. In E. Gellert (Ed.), *Psychosocial aspects of pediatric care* (pp. 37-49). New York: Grune & Stratton.

Bates, B. (1970). Doctor and nurse: Changing roles and relations. *New England Journal of Medicine, 283,* 129-134.

Bauer, R., Harper, R., & Kenny, T. (1974). Treatment for uncontrolled juvenile diabetes. *Journal of Pediatric Psychology, 2,* 2-3.

Beales, J. G. (1982). The assessment and management of pain in children. In P. Karoly, J. J. Steffen, & D. J. O'Grady (Eds.), *Child health psychology: Concepts and issues* (pp. 154-179). New York: Pergamon.

Beezley, P., Martin, H., & Alexander, H. (1976). Comprehensive family oriented therapy. In R. E. Helfer & C. H. Kempe (Eds.), *Child abuse and neglect: The family and the community* (pp. 169-194). Cambridge, MA: Ballinger.

Bergner, R., & Bergner, A. (1976). Rational asthma therapy for the outpatient. *Journal of the American Medical Association, 235,* 288-293.

Bernstein, N. R. (1965). Observations on the use of hypnosis with burned children on a pediatric ward. *The International Journal of Clinical and Experimental Hypnosis, 13,* 1-10.

Beyer, J. E., DeGood, D. E., Ashley, L. C., & Russell, G. A. (1983). Patterns of postoperative analgesic use with adults and children following cardiac surgery. *Pain, 17,* 71-81.

Bibace, R., & Walsh, N. E. (1980). Development of children's concepts of illness. *Pediatrics, 66,* 912-917.

Bird, B. L. (1982). Behavioral interventions in pediatric neurology. In D. C. Russo & J. W. Varni (Eds.), *Behavioral pediatrics: Research and practice* (pp. 101-142). New York: Plenum.

Blount, R. L., Dahlquist, L. M., Baer, R. A., & Wuori, D. (1984). A brief, effective method for teaching children to swallow pills. *Behavior Therapy, 15,* 381-387.

Bluebond-Langer, M. (1974). I know, do you? A study of awareness, communication, and coping in terminally ill children. In B. Schoenberg, A. Carr, D. Peretz, & A. Kutscher (Eds.), *Anticipatory grief* (pp. 171-181). New York: Columbia University Press.

Bluebond-Langer, M. (1977). Meanings of death to children. In H. Feifel (Ed.), *New meanings of death* (pp. 47-66). New York: McGraw-Hill.

Botvin, G. J., & Eng, A. (1980). A comprehensive school-based smoking prevention program. *The Journal of School Health, 50,* 209-213.

Botvin, G. J., & Eng, A. (1982). The efficacy of a multi-component approach to the prevention of cigarette smoking. *Preventive Medicine, 11,* 199-211.

Bowlby, J. (1982). *Attachment and loss: Vol. 1. Attachment.* New York: Basic.

Brain, D. J., & Maclay, I. (1968). Controlled study of mothers and children in hospital. *British Medical Journal, 1,* 278-280.

Brazelton, T. B. (1975). Anticipatory guidance. *Pediatric Clinics of North America, 22,* 533-544.

Brennemann, J. (1931). The menace of psychiatry. *American Journal of Diseases of Children, 42,* 376-402.

Brewster, A. (1982). Chronically ill hospitalized children's concepts of their illness. *Pediatrics, 69,* 355-362.

Bricker, W. A., & Bricker, D. D. (1976). The Infant, Toddler and Preschool Research and Intervention Project. In T. Tjossem (Ed.), *Intervention and strategies for high risk infants and young children* (pp. 545-572). Baltimore: University Park.

Bronfenbrenner, U. (1979). *The ecology of human development: Experiments by nature and design.* Cambridge, MA: Harvard University Press.

Brown, J. K. (1977). Migraine and migraine equivalents in children. *Developmental Medicine and Child Neurology, 19,* 683-692.

Brownell, K. D., & Kaye, F. S. (1982). A school-based behavior modification, nutrition education, and physical activity program for obese children. *American Journal of Clinical Nutrition, 35,* 277-283.

Brownlee-Duffeck, M., Peterson, L., Simonds, J. F., Goldstein, D., Kilo, C., & Hoett, N. (1987). The role of health beliefs in the regimen adherence and metabolic control of adolescents and adults with diabetes mellitus. *Journal of Consulting and Clinical Psychology, 55,* 139-144.

Brucefors, A. (1972, Spring). *Trends in development of abilities.* Paper presented at Reunion de Coordination des Recherches sur la Croissance et le Development de l'Enfant, Normal, Institute of Child Health, London.

Brunk, M., Henggeler, S. W., & Whelan, J. P. (1987). Comparison of multisystemic therapy and parent training in the brief treatment of child abuse and neglect. *Journal of Consulting and Clinical Psychology, 55,* 171-178.

Burbach, D. J., & Peterson, L. (1986). Children's concepts of physical illness: A review and critique of the cognitive developmental literature. *Health Psychology, 5,* 307-325.

Burstein, S., & Meichenbaum, D. (1979). The work of worrying in children undergoing surgery. *Journal of Abnormal Child Psychology, 7,* 121-132.

Bush, J. P., Melamed, B. G., Sheras, P. L., & Greenbaum, P. E. (1986). Mother-child patterns of coping with anticipatory medical stress. *Health Psychology, 5,* 137-157.

Carney, R. M., Schechter, K., & Davis, T. (1983). Improving adherence to blood glucose testing in insulin-dependent diabetic children. *Behavior Therapy, 14,* 247-254.

Cassell, S. (1965). Effects of brief puppet therapy upon the emotional responses of children undergoing cardiac catheterization. *Journal of Consulting and Clinical Psychology, 29,* 1-8.

Cataldo, M. F., Bessman, C. A., Parker, L. H., Pearson, J. E. R., & Rogers, M. C. (1979). Behavioral assessment for pediatric intensive care units. *Journal of Applied Behavior Analysis, 12,* 83-97.

Center for the Improvement of Child Caring. (1977). *Save the children*. Los Angeles, CA: Author.

Chan, D. A., Salcedo, J. R., Atkins, D. M., & Ruley, E. J. (1986). Munchausen Syndrome by Proxy: A review and case study. *Journal of Pediatric Psychology, 11*, 71-80.

Chan, J. M. (1980). Preparation for procedures and surgery through play. *Paediatrician, 9*, 210-219.

Chapman, A. H., Loeb, D. G., & Gibbons, M. J. (1956). Psychiatric aspects of hospitalizing children. *Archives of Pediatrics, 73*, 77-88.

Christophersen, E. R. (1977). *Little people: Guidelines for common sense child rearing*. Lawrence, KS: H & H Enterprises.

Citrin, W. S., Zigo, M. A., La Greca, A. M., & Skyler, J. S. (1982, June). *Diabetes in adolescence: Effects of multifamily group therapy and parent simulation of diabetes*. Paper presented at the meeting of the American Diabetes Association, San Francisco.

Claerhout, S., & Lutzker, J. R. (1981). Increasing children's self-initiated compliance to dental regimens. *Behavior Therapy, 12*, 164-176.

Clark, G. D., Key, J. D., Rutherford, P., & Bithoney, W. G. (1984). Munchausen's Syndrome by Proxy (child abuse) presenting as apparent autoerythrocyte sensitization syndrome: An unusual presentation of Polle Syndrome. *Pediatrics, 74*, 1100-1102.

Clarke, A. M. (1980). Thermal injuries: The care of the whole child. *The Journal of Trauma, 20*, 823-829.

Coates, T. J., Jeffrey, R. W., Slinkard, L. A., Killen, J. D., & Danaher, B. G. (1982). Frequency of contact and monetary reward in weight loss, lipid changes, and blood pressure reduction with adolescents. *Behavior Therapy, 13*, 175-185.

Cole, N. S. (1981). Bias in testing. *American Psychologist, 36*, 1067-1077.

Collier, B. N., & Etzwiler, D. D. (1971). Comparative study of diabetes knowledge among juvenile diabetics and their parents. *Diabetes, 20*, 51-57.

Collins, A. M., & Quillian, M. R. (1972). How to make a language user. In E. Tulving & W. Donaldson (Eds.), *Organization and memory* (pp. 210-260). New York: Academic.

Colver, A. F., Hutchinson, P. J., & Judson, E. C. (1982). Promoting children's home safety. *British Medical Journal, 285*, 1177-1180.

Conrad, P. (1975). The discovery of hyperkinesis: Notes on the medicalization of deviant behavior. *Social Problems, 23*, 12-21.

Cook, S. (1975). *The development of causal thinking with regard to physical illness among French children*. Unpublished doctoral dissertation, University of Kansas, Kansas City.

Coppens, N. M. (1985). Cognitive development and locus of control as predictors of preschoolers' understanding of safety and prevention. *Journal of Applied Developmental Psychology, 6*, 43-55.

Cott, A., Pavloski, R. D., & Black, A. H. (1979). Reducing epileptic seizures through operant conditioning of central nervous system activity: Procedural variables. *Science, 203,* 73-75.

Crittenden, M., & Gofman, H. (1976). Follow-ups and downs: The medical center, the family, and the school. *Journal of Pediatric Psychology, 1,* 66-68.

Crocker, E. (1979). Hospital books for children. *Canadian Nurse, 75,* 33.

Crowl, M. (1980). Case study: The basic process of art therapy as demonstrated by efforts to allay a child's fear of surgery. *American Journal of Art Therapy, 19,* 49-51.

Cyphert, F. R. (1973). Back to school for the child with cancer. *Journal of School Health, 43,* 215-217.

Davidson, C. (1988). Training the pediatric psychologist and the behavioral pediatrician. In D. K. Routh (Ed.), *Handbook of pediatric psychology* (pp. 507-537). New York: Guilford.

Davis, J. (1972). NIAID initiatives in allergy research. *Journal of Allergy, 49,* 323-382.

DeLong, D. R. (1971). *Individual differences in patterns of anxiety arousal, stress-relevant information and recovery from surgery.* Unpublished doctoral dissertation, University of California, Los Angeles.

Derschewitz, R. A., & Williamson, J. W. (1977). Prevention of childhood household injuries: A controlled clinical trial. *American Journal of Public Health, 67,* 1148-1153.

Dielman, T. E., Leech, S. L., Becker, M. H., Rosenstock, I. M., & Horvath, W. J. (1980). Dimensions of children's health beliefs. *Health Education Quarterly, 7,* 219-238.

Dietrich, S. L. (1976). Musculoskeletal problems. In M. W. Hilgartner (Ed.), *Hemophilia in children* (pp. 59-70). Littleton, MA: Publishing Sciences Group.

Dimick, A. R. (1977). An overview. In Ethical Communications, Inc. (Eds.), *Practical approaches to burn management* (p. 1). Deerfield, IL: Flint Laboratories.

Doleys, D. M. (1977). Behavioral treatments for nocturnal enuresis in children: A review of the recent literature. *Psychological Bulletin, 84,* 30-54.

Doleys, D. M. (1979). Assessment and treatment of childhood enuresis. In A. J. Finch & P. C. Kendall (Eds.), *Chemical treatment and research in child psychopathology* (pp. 207-233). New York: Spectrum.

Dolovich, J., Hargreave, L., & Wilson, W. (1975). Control of asthma in children. *Primary Care, 2,* 19-38.

Douglas, J. W. B. (1975). Early hospital admission and later disturbances of behavior and learning. *Developmental Medicine and Child Neurology, 17,* 456-480.

Drotar, D. (1976). Psychological consultation in a pediatric hospital. *Professional Psychology, 7,* 77-83.

Drotar, D. (1977). Clinical psychological practice in a pediatric hospital. *Professional Psychology, 8,* 72-80.

Drotar, D. (1978). Training psychologists to consult with pediatricians: Problems and prospects. *Journal of Clinical Child Psychology, 7,* 57-60.

Drotar, D. (1982). The child psychologist in the medical system. In P. Karoly, J. J. Steffen, & D. J. O'Grady (Eds.), *Child health psychology: Concepts and issues* (pp. 1-28). New York: Pergamon.

Drotar, D. (1983). Transacting with physicians: Fact and fiction. *Journal of Pediatric Psychology, 8,* 117-127.

Drotar, D., Benjamin, P., Chwast, R., Litt, C., & Vajner, P. (1982). The role of the psychologist in pediatric outpatient and inpatient settings. In J. Tuma (Ed.), *Handbook for the practice of pediatric psychology* (pp. 228-250). New York: Wiley.

Drotar, D., Crawford, P., & Ganofsky, M. A. (1984). Prevention with chronically ill children. In M. C. Roberts & L. Peterson (Eds.), *Prevention of problems in childhood: Psychological research and applications* (pp. 232-265). New York: Wiley.

Drotar, D., & Malone, C. A. (1982). Psychological consultation on a pediatric infant division. *Journal of Pediatric Psychology, 7*(1), 23-32.

Drotar, D., Malone, C. A., & Negray, J. (1980). Intellectual assessment of young children with environmentally based failure to thrive. *Child Abuse and Neglect, 4,* 23-31.

Drotar, D., Malone, C. M., Negray, J., & Dennstedt, M. (1983). Psychosocial assessment and care of infants hospitalized for nonorganic failure to thrive. *Child Abuse and Neglect: The International Journal, 3,* 927-935.

Duffy, J. C. (1977). *Child psychiatry: Medical outline series.* Flushing, NY: Medical Examination Publishing.

Eckenhoff, J. F. (1953). Preanesthetic sedation for children: Analysis of the effects for tonsillectomy and adenoidectomy. *American Medical Association Archives of Otolaryngology, 57,* 411-416.

Ehrlich, R. M. (1974). Diabetes mellitus in childhood. *Pediatric Clinics of North America, 21,* 871-884.

Eland, J. M. (1981). Minimizing pain associated with prekindergarten intramuscular injections. *Issues in Comprehensive Pediatric Nursing, 5,* 361-372.

Eland, J. M., & Anderson, J. E. (1977). The experience of pain in children. In A. Jacox (Ed.), *Pain: A source book for nurses and other professionals* (pp. 453-473). Boston: Little, Brown.

Elliott, C. H., & Olson, R. A. (1983). The management of children's distress in response to painful medical treatment for burn injuries. *Behavior Research and Therapy, 21,* 675-683.

Ellison, P. H., Largent, J. A., & Bahr, J. P. (1981). A scoring system to predict outcome following neonatal seizures. *Journal of Pediatrics, 99,* 455-459.

Elmer, E., & Gregg, G. S. (1967). Developmental characteristics of abused children. *Pediatrics, 40,* 596-602.

Epstein, L. H., Beck, S., Figueroa, J., Farkas, G., Kazdin, A. E., Daneman, D., & Becker, D. (1981). The effects of targeting improvements in urine glucose on metabolic control in children with insulin dependent diabetes. *Journal of Applied Behavior Analysis, 14,* 365-375.

Epstein, L. H., Cobrun, C., Becker, D., Drash, A., & Siminerio, L. (1980). Measurement and modification of the accuracy of determinations of urine glucose concentration. *Diabetes Care, 3,* 535-536.

Epstein, L. H., Masek, B. J., & Marshall, W. R. (1978). A nutritionally based school program for control of eating in obese children. *Behavior Therapy, 9,* 766-778.

Epstein, L. H., Wing, R. R., Steranchak, L., Dickson, B., & Michelson, J. (1980). Comparison of family-based behavior modification and nutrition education for childhood obesity. *Journal of Pediatric Psychology, 5,* 25-36.

Ernst, A. R., Routh, D. K., & Harper, D. C. (1984). Abdominal pain in children and symptoms of somatization disorder. *Journal of Pediatric Psychology, 9,* 77-86.

Evans, R. I., Rozelle, R. M., Lasater, T. M., Dembroski, T. M., & Allen, B. P. (1968). New measure of effects of persuasive communications: A chemical indicator of toothbrushing behavior. *Psychological Reports, 23,* 731-736.

Evans, R. I., Rozelle, R. M., Lasater, T. M., Dembroski, T. M., & Allen, B. P. (1970). Fear arousal, persuasion, and actual versus implied behavior change: New perspective utilizing a real-life dental hygiene program. *Journal of Personality and Social Psychology, 16,* 220-227.

Evans, R. I., Rozelle, R. M., Mittlemark, M. B., Hansen, W. B., Bane, A. L., & Havis, J. (1978). Deterring the onset of smoking in children: Knowledge of immediate physiological effects and coping with peer pressure, media pressure, and parent modeling. *Journal of Applied Social Psychology, 8,* 126-135.

Eyberg, S. M. (1974). *Manual for coding dyadic parent-child interactions.* Unpublished manuscript, Oregon Health Sciences University, Department of Medical Psychology, Portland.

Eyberg, S. M. (1985). Behavioral assessment: Advancing methodology in pediatric psychology. *Journal of Pediatric Psychology, 10,* 123-139.

Faust, D. S., Ulissi, S. M., & Thurber, S. (1980). Postdoctoral training opportunities in pediatric psychology: A review. *Journal of Pediatric Psychology, 5,* 277-286.

Fehrenbach, A. B., & Peterson, L. (1983, August). *Parental problem solving, stress, and dietary compliance in P.K.U. children.* Paper presented at the meeting of the American Psychological Association, Anaheim, CA.

Feinstein, H. N. (1964). Group therapy for mothers with infanticidal impulses. *American Journal of Psychiatry, 120,* 882-886.

Feldman, G. (1976). The effect of biofeedback training on respiratory resistance of asthmatic children. *Psychosomatic Medicine, 38,* 27-34.

Ferguson, B. F. (1979). Preparing young children for hospitalization: A comparison of two methods. *Pediatrics, 64,* 656-664.

Fernald, C. D., & Corry, J. J. (1981). Empathetic versus directive preparation of children for needles. *Journal of the Association for the Care of Children's Health, 10,* 44-47.

Field, T. M. (1977). Effects of early separation, interactive deficit, and experimental manipulations on infant-mother face-to-face interaction. *Child Development, 48,* 763-771.

Field, T. M. (1982). Infants born at risk: Early compensatory experiences. In L. A. Bond & J. M. Joffe (Eds.), *Facilitating infant and early development* (pp. 309-342). Hanover, NH: University Press of New England.

Finley, W. W. (1976). Effects of sham feedback following successful SMR training in an epileptic: Follow-up study. *Biofeedback and Self-Regulation, 1,* 227-235.

Finley, W. W., Niman, C. A., Standley, J., & Wansley, R. A. (1977). Electrophysiologic behavior modification of frontal EMG in cerebral-palsied children. *Biofeedback and Self-Regulation, 2,* 59-79.

Follansbee, D. J., La Greca, A. M., & Citrin, W. S. (1983, June). *Coping skills training for adolescents with diabetes.* Paper presented at the meeting of the American Diabetes Association, San Antonio, TX.

Fontana, V. J. (1973). *Somewhere a child is crying: Maltreatment—Causes and prevention.* New York: Macmillan.

Franz, I. D. (1913). On psychology and medical education. *Science, 38,* 555-566.

Freiman, J., & Buchanan, N. (1978). Drug compliance and therapeutic considerations in 75 black epileptic children. *Central African Journal of Medicine, 24,* 136-140.

Friedman, S. B., & Phillips, S. (1981). What's the difference? Pediatric residents and their inaccurate concepts regarding statistics. *Pediatrics, 68,* 644-646.

Gabriel, H. P. (1977). A practical approach to preparing children for dermatologic surgery. *Journal of Dermatological Surgery and Oncology, 3,* 523-526.

Gabriel, H. P., & Danilowicz, D. (1978). Postoperative responses in "prepared" child after cardiac surgery. *British Heart Journal, 40,* 1046-1051.

Gaines, R., Sandgrund, A., Green, A. H., & Power, E. (1978). Etiological factors in child maltreatment: A multivariate study of abusing, neglecting, and normal mothers. *Journal of Abnormal Psychology, 87,* 531-540.

Ganofsky, M. A. (1981). Advocacy in the schools. *Council of Nephrology Social Work Newsletter, 6,* 3-4.

Gardner, J. (1967). Behavior therapy treatment approach to a psychogenic seizure case. *Journal of Consulting Psychology, 31,* 209-212.

Gardner, R. A. (1977). *The parent's book about divorce.* New York: Doubleday.

Garling, T., & Valsinger, J. (Eds.). (1986). *Children within environments: Toward a psychology of accident prevention.* New York: Plenum.

Garner, A. M., & Thompson, C. W. (1978). Juvenile diabetes. In P. R. Magrab (Ed.), *Psychological management of pediatric problems* (Vol. 1, pp. 221-258). Baltimore: University Park Press.

Garrard, S. D., & Richmond, J. B. (1963). Psychological aspects of the management of chronic diseases and handicapping conditions in childhood. In H. E. Lief, V. F. Lief, & N. R. Lief (Eds.), *The psychological basis of medical practice* (pp. 370-403). New York: Harper & Row.

Gastaut, H. (1970). Clinical and electroencephalographic classification of epileptic seizures. *Epilepsia, 11,* 102-113.

Gatch, G. (1982). Caring for children needing anesthesia. *AORN Journal, 35,* 218-226.

Geist, R. (1977). Consultation on a pediatric surgical ward: Creating an empathic climate. *American Journal of Orthopsychiatry, 47,* 432-444.

Gelfand, D. M., & Peterson, L. (1985). *Child development and child psychopathology.* Beverly Hills, CA: Sage.

Georgeopollous, B. S., & Mann, F. C. (1979). The hospital as an organization. In E. G. Jaco (Ed.), *Patients, physicians, and illness* (pp. 296-305). New York: Macmillan.

Gershen, J. A. (1976). Maternal influence on the behavior patterns of children in the dental situation. *Journal of Dentistry for Children, 43,* 28-32.

Gilbert, B. O., Johnson, S. B., Spillar, R., McCallum, M., Silverstein, J. H., & Rosenbloom, A. (1982). The effects of a peer-modeling film on children learning to self-inject insulin. *Behavior Therapy, 13,* 186-193.

Ginther, L. J., & Roberts, M. C. (1982). A test of mastery versus coping modeling in the reduction of children's dental fears. *Child and Family Behavior Therapy, 4,* 41-51.

Gogan, J. L., O'Malley, J. E., & Foster, D. J. (1977). Treating the pediatric cancer patient: A review. *Journal of Pediatric Psychology, 2,* 42-48.

Gordon, N. (1978). Duration of treatment for childhood epilepsy. *Developmental Medicine and Child Neurology, 24,* 84-88.

Goslin, E. R. (1978). Hospitalization as a life crisis for the pre-school child: A critical review. *Journal of Community Health, 3,* 321-346.

Gray, J. J. (1979). Positive reinforcement and punishment in the treatment of childhood trichotillomania. *Journal of Behavior Therapy and Experimental Psychiatry, 10,* 125-129.

Green, M. (1967). Diagnosis and treatment: Psychogenic, recurrent abdominal pain. *Pediatrics, 40*(1), 84-89.

Green, M., & Hoelkelman, R. A. (1982). Trends in the education of pediatricians. *Advances in Pediatrics, 29,* 325-349.

Greene, P. (1975). The child with leukemia in the classroom. *American Journal of Nursing, 75,* 86-87.

Gross, A. M., Stern, R. M., Levin, R. B., Dale, J., & Wojnilower, D. A. (1983). The effect of mother-child separation on the behavior of children experiencing a diagnostic medical procedure. *Journal of Consulting and Clinical Psychology, 51,* 783-785.

Haddon, W., Jr. (1984). Preface. In S. P. Baker, B. O'Neill, & R. S. Karpf. *The injury fact book* (pp. xxxi-xxxii). Lexington, MA: Lexington.

Haimowitz, M. L. (1972). Thoughts on helping the patient with diabetes. *Journal of the American Dietetic Association, 61,* 425-428.

Handford, H. A., Charney, D., Ackerman, L., Eyster, M. E., & Bixler, E. O. (1980). Effect of psychiatric intervention on use of antihemophilic factor concentrate. *American Journal of Psychiatry, 137,* 1254-1256.

Hanson, C. L., Henggeler, S. W., & Burghen, G. A. (1987). Social competence and parental support as mediators of the link between stress and metabolic control in adolescents with insulin-dependent diabetes mellitus. *Journal of Consulting and Clinical Psychology, 55,* 529-533.

Hardgrove, C. B. (1980). Helping parents on the pediatric ward: A report on a survey of hospitals with "Living-In" programs. *Paediatrician, 9,* 220-223.

Harper, D. C., Wacker, D. P., & Cobb, L. S. (1986). Children's social preferences toward peers with visible physical differences. *Journal of Pediatric Psychology, 11,* 323-342.

Hartup, W. W. (1979). Peer relations and the growth of social competence. In M. W. Kent & J. E. Rolf (Eds.), *Primary prevention of psychopathology: Social competence in children* (Vol. 3, pp. 150-170). Hanover, NH: University Press of New England.

Hartup, W. W. (1983). Peer relations. In P. H. Mussen (Ed.), *Handbook of child psychology* (Vol. 4, pp. 103-196). New York: Wiley.

Harvey, S. (1980). The value of play through therapy in hospital. *Paediatrician, 9,* 191-198.

Hedberg, A. G., & Schlong, A. (1973). Eliminating fainting by school children during mass inoculation clinics. *Nursing Research, 22,* 352-353.

Heffernan, M., & Azarnoff, P. (1971). Factors in reducing children's anxiety about clinic visits. *Health Services and Mental Health Administration Health Reports, 86,* 1131-1135.

Helfer, R. E. (1975). *Child abuse and neglect: The diagnostic process and treatment programs* (OHD Publication No. 75-69). Washington, DC: United States Department of Health, Education, and Welfare.

Hitchcock, L. S. (1982). *Improving recovery from surgery: The interaction of preoperative interventions, coping processes, and personality variables.* Unpublished doctoral dissertation, University of Texas, Austin.

Hodges, K., Kline, J., Barbero, G., & Flanery, R. (1984). Life events occurring in families of children with recurrent abdominal pain. *Journal of Psychosomatic Research, 28,* 185-188.

Hodges, K., Kline, J., Fitch, P., McKnew, D., & Cytryn, L. (1981). The child assessment schedule: A diagnostic interview for research and clinical use. *Catalog of Selected Documents in Psychology, 11,* 56.

Hoelscher, T. J., & Lichstein, K. L. (1984). Behavioral assessment and treatment of child migraine: Implications for clinical research and practice. *Headache, 24,* 94-103.

Hops, H., & Greenwood, G. R. (1981). Social skills deficit. In E. J. Mash & L. G. Terdal (Eds.), *Behavioral assessment of childhood disorders* (pp. 347-397). New York: Guilford.

Hostler, S. I. (1978). The development of the child's concept of death. In O. J. Z. Sahler (Ed.), *The child and death* (pp. 1-25). St. Louis: Mosby.

Hughes, M. C. (1984). Recurrent abdominal pain and childhood depression: Clinical observations of 23 children and their families. *American Journal of Orthopsychiatry, 54,* 146-155.

Hughes, M. C., & Zimin, R. (1978). Children with psychogenic abdominal pain and their families. *Clinical Pediatrics, 17,* 569-573.

Hurd, P. D., Johnson, C. A., Pechacek, F., Bast, L. P., Jacobs, D. R., & Luepker, R. V. (1980). Prevention of cigarette smoking in seventh grade students. *Journal of Behavioral Medicine, 3,* 15-28.

Ince, L. D. (1976). The use of relaxation training and a conditioned stimulus in the elimination of epileptic seizures in a child: A case study. *Journal of Behavior Therapy and Experimental Psychiatry, 7,* 39-42.

Jay, G. W., & Tomasi, L. G. (1981). Pediatric headaches: A one year retrospective analysis. *Headache, 21,* 5-9.

Jay, S. M., Elliott, C. H., Katz, E., & Siegel, S. E. (1987). Cognitive behavioral and pharmacologic interventions for children's distress during painful medical procedures: A treatment outcome study. *Journal of Consulting and Clinical Psychology, 55,* 860-865.

Jay, S. M., Elliott, C. H., Ozolins, M., & Olson, R. (1983). *Behavioral management of children's distress during painful medical procedures.* Unpublished manuscript.

Jay, S. M., Ozolins, N., Elliott, C. H., & Caldwell, S. (1983). Assessment of children's distress during painful medical procedures. *Health Psychology, 2,* 133-147.

Jette, A. M. (1980). Functional status index: Reliability of a chronic disease evaluation instrument. *Archives of Physical Medicine and Rehabilitation, 61,* 395-401.

Johnson, J. E., Kirchoff, K. T., & Endress, M. D. (1975). Altering children's distress behavior during orthopedic cast removal. *Nursing Research, 24,* 404-410.

Johnson, M. R. (1979). Mental health interventions with medically ill children: A review of the literature 1970-1977. *Journal of Pediatric Psychology, 4,* 147-164.

Johnson, S. B. (1984). Knowledge, attitudes, and behavior: Correlates of health in childhood diabetes. *Clinical Psychology Review, 4,* 503-524.

Johnson, S. B., Pollak, T., Silverstein, J. H., Rosenbloom, A. L., Spillar, R., McCallum, M., & Harkavy, J. (1982). Cognitive and behavioral knowledge about insulin dependent diabetes among children and parents. *Pediatrics, 69,* 708-713.

Johnston, M., & Salazar, M. (1979). Preadmission program for rehospitalized children. *American Journal of Nursing, 79,* 1420-1422.

Johnston, M. V., & Freeman, J. M. (1981). Pharmacologic advances in seizure control. *Pediatric Clinics of North America, 28,* 179-194.

Jones, R. T., Kazdin, A. E., & Haney, J. I. (1981). Social validation and training of emergency fire safety skills for potential injury prevention and life saving. *Journal of Applied Behavior Analysis, 14,* 249-260.

Jones, S. T. (1985a). Reducing children's psychological stress in the operating suite. *Opthalmic Plastic and Reconstruction Surgery, 1,* 199-203.

Jones, S. T. (1985b). Unnecessary psychological complications in children after surgery. *Journal of Pediatric Opthalmology and Strabismus, 22,* 218-220.

Jovanovic, L., & Peterson, C. M. (1981). The clinical utility of glycosylated hemoglobin. In J. S. Skyler & G. F. Cahill, Jr. (Eds.), *Diabetes mellitus* (pp. 165-172). New York: Yorke Medical.

Justice, B., & Justice, R. (1976). *The abusing family.* New York: Human Sciences.

Kagan, J. (1965). The new marriage: Pediatrics and psychology. *American Journal of Diseases of Childhood, 110,* 272-278.

Kaplan, D. M., Smith, A., & Grobstein, R. (1974). School management of the seriously ill child. *Journal of School Health, 44,* 250-254.

Karoly, P. (1982). Developmental pediatrics: A process-oriented approach to the analysis of health competence. In P. Karoly, J. J. Steffen, & D. J. O'Grady (Eds.), *Child health psychology: Concepts and issues* (pp. 29-57). New York: Pergamon.

Karp, M., & Teuscher, G. W. (1947). General anesthesia in difficult pedodontic patients. *Journal of Pediatrics, 30,* 317-323.

Kass, E. R., Sigman, M., Bromwich, R. F., & Parmelee, A. H. (1976). Educational intervention with high risk infants and young children. In T. Tjossem (Ed.), *Intervention strategies for high risk infants and young children* (pp. 535-644). Baltimore: University Park Press.

Katz, E. R. (1980). Illness impact and social reintegration. In J. Kellerman (Ed.), *Psychological aspects of childhood cancer* (pp. 14-46). Springfield, IL: Thomas.

Katz, E. R., Kellerman, J., Rigler, D., Williams, K. O., & Siegel, S. E. (1977). School intervention with pediatric cancer patients. *Journal of Pediatric Psychology, 2*(2), 72-76.

Katz, E. R., Kellerman, J., & Siegel, S. E. (1980). Behavioral distress in children with cancer undergoing medical procedures: Developmental considerations. *Journal of Consulting and Clinical Psychology, 48,* 356-365.

Kazdin, A. E., Moser, J., Colbus, D., & Bell, R. (1985). Depressive symptoms among physically abused and psychiatrically disturbed children. *Journal of Consulting and Clinical Psychology, 94,* 298-307.

Kearsley, R. B. (1981). Cognitive assessment of the handicapped infant: The need for an alternative approach. *American Journal of Orthopsychiatry, 51*(1), 43-54.

Kellerman, I., Rigler, D., & Siegel, S. E. (1979). Psychological response of children to isolation in a protected environment. *Journal of Behavioral Medicine, 2,* 263-276.

Kellerman, J., Zeltzer, L., Ellenberg, L., & Dash, J. (1983). Adolescents with cancer: Hypnosis for the reduction of the acute pain and anxiety associated with medical procedures. *Journal of Adolescent Health Care, 4,* 85-90.

Kelley, M. L., Jarvie, G. J., Middlebrook, J. L., McNeer, M. F., & Drabman, R. S. (1984). Descreasing burned children's pain behavior: Impacting the trauma of hydrotherapy. *Journal of Applied Behavior Analysis, 17,* 147-158.

Kempe, C. H., & Helfer, R. E. (1972). *Helping the battered child and his family.* Philadelphia: Lippincott.

Kinard, E. M. (1982). Experiencing child abuse: Effects on emotional adjustment. *American Journal of Orthopsychiatry, 52,* 82-91.

Klackenberg-Larsson, I., & Stensson, J. (1968). Data on the mental development during the first five years. *Acta Paediatrica Scandinavica, 57* (Suppl. 187), 67-93.

Klaus, M. H., & Kennell, J. K. (1982). *Maternal-infant bonding.* St. Louis: Mosby.

Klein, M., & Stern, L. (1971). Low birth weight and the battered child syndrome. *American Journal of Disabled Children, 122,* 15-18.

Klorman, R., Hilpert, P. L., Michael, R., LaGana, C., & Sveen, O. B. (1980). Effects of coping and mastery modeling on experienced and inexperienced pedodontic patients' disruptiveness. *Behavior Therapy, 11,* 156-168.

Knight, R. B., Atkins, A., Eagle, C., Evans, N., Finkelstein, J. W., Fukushima, D., Katz, J., & Weiner, H. (1979). Psychological stress, ego defenses, and cortisol production in children hospitalized for elective surgery. *Psychosomatic Medicine, 41,* 40-49.

Koocher, G. P. (1973). Childhood, death, and cognitive development. *Developmental Psychology, 9,* 369-375.

Koocher, G. P. (1984). Coping with survivorship in childhood cancer: Family problems. In A. E. Christ & K. Flomenhaft (Eds.), *Childhood cancer: Impact on the family* (pp. 203-212). New York: Plenum.

Koocher, G. P., & Sallan, S. E. (1982). Pediatric oncology. In P. R. Magrab (Ed.), *Psychological management of pediatric problems* (Vol. 1, pp. 283-307). Baltimore: University Park Press.

Koocher, G. P., Sourkes, B. M., & Keane, W. M. (1979). Pediatric oncology consultations: A generalizable model for medical settings. *Professional Psychology, 10,* 467-474.

Korsch, B. M. (1961). Psychologic reactions to physical illness in children. *107th Annual Session of the Medical Association of Georgia, Atlanta, 50,* 519-523.

Korsch, B. M., Cobb, K., & Ashe, B. (1961). Pediatricians' appraisals of patients' intelligence. *Pediatrics, 27,* 990-1003.

Koski, M. L. (1969). The coping processes in childhood diabetes. *Acta Paediatrica Scandinavica, 58* (Suppl. 198), 7-56.

Kucera, J. (1971). Leukemia and twinning tendency in families of children with Down's syndrome. *Journal of Mental Deficiency Research, 15,* 77-80.

Kucia, C., Drotar, D., Doershuk, C. F., Stern, R. C., Boat, T. F., & Mathews, L. (1979). Home observation of family interaction and childhood adjustment to cystic fibrosis. *Journal of Pediatric Psychology, 4,* 189-195.

Kuhlman, W. N. (1978). EEG feedback training of epileptic patients: Clinical and electroencephalographic analysis. *Electroencephalography and Clinical Neurophysiology, 45,* 699-710.

LaBaw, W., Holton, C., Tewell, K., & Eccles, D. (1975). The use of self-hypnosis by children with cancer. *The American Journal of Clinical Hypnosis, 17,* 233-238.

Labbé, E. E., & Williamson, D. A. (1983). Temperature biofeedback in the treatment of children with migraine headaches. *Journal of Pediatric Psychology, 8,* 317-325.

Ladd, G. W., & Mize, J. (1983). A cognitive-social learning model of social-skills training. *Psychological Review, 90,* 127-157.

La Greca, A. M. (1982, June). *Behavioral aspects of diabetes management in children and adolescents.* Paper presented at the meeting of the American Diabetes Association, San Francisco.

La Greca, A. M. (1988a). Adherence to prescribed medical regimens. In D. K. Routh (Ed.), *Handbook of pediatric psychology* (pp. 299-320). New York: Guilford.

La Greca, A. M. (1988b). Children with diabetes and their families: Coping and disease management. In T. Field, P. McCabe, & N. Schneiderman (Eds.), *Stress and coping* (Vol. 2, pp 139-164). Englewood Cliffs, NJ: Erlbaum.

La Greca, A. M., & Hanna, N. C. (1983, June). *Health beliefs of children and their mothers: Implications for treatment.* Paper presented at the meeting of the American Diabetes Association, San Antonio, TX.

La Greca, A. M., & Ottinger, D. R. (1979). Self-monitoring and relaxation training in the treatment of medically ordered exercises in a 12-year-old female. *Journal of Pediatric Psychology, 4,* 49-54.

Lake, C. R., Mikkelsen, E. J., Rapport, J. L., Zavadil, A. P., & Kopin, I. J. (1979). Effect of imipramine on norepinephrine and blood pressure in enuretic boys. *Clinical Pharmacology and Therapeutics, 26,* 647-653.

Lambert, L. (1984). Variables that affect the school-age child's reaction to hospitalization and surgery: A review of the literature. *Maternal Child Nursing Journal, 13,* 1-18.

Lamontagne, L. L. (1984). Children's locus of control beliefs as predictors of preoperative coping behavior. *Nursing Research, 33,* 76-79, 85.

Lane, V. W., & Samples, J. M. (1984). Tuberous sclerosis: Case study of early seizure control and subsequent normal development. *Journal of Autism and Developmental Disorders, 14,* 423-427.

Lansky, S. B., Cairns, N. V., Hassanein, R., Wehr, J., & Lowman, J. T. (1978). Childhood cancer: Parental discord and divorce. *Pediatrics, 62,* 184-188.

Lansky, S. B., Lowman, J. T., & Gyulay, J. (1975). School phobia in children with malignant neoplasms. *American Journal of Diseases of Children, 129,* 42-46.

Lask, B., & Kirk, M. (1979). Childhood asthma: Family therapy as an adjunct to routine management. *Journal of Family Therapy, 1,* 33-49.

Lattal, K. A. (1969). Contingency management of toothbrushing behavior in a summer camp for children. *Journal of Applied Behavior Analysis, 2,* 195-198.

Lebaw, W. L. (1970). Regular use of suggestibility by pediatric bleeders. *Haematologia, 4,* 419-425.

Lebaw, W. L. (1975). Autohypnosis in haemophilia. *Haematologia, 9,* 103-110.

Levine, S. (1980). A coping model of mother-infant relationships. In S. Levine & U. Ursin (Eds.), *Coping and health* (pp. 87-100). New York: Plenum.

Levinson, P., & Ousterhout, D. K. (1980). Art and play therapy with pediatric burn patients. *Journal of Burn Care and Rehabilitation, 1,* 42-46.

Lewis, M. (Ed.). (1976). *Origins of intelligence: Infancy and early childhood.* New York: Plenum.

Lewis, M. (1979). Psychology. In P. J. Valetutti & F. Christoples (Eds.), *Preventing physical and mental disabilities: Multi-disciplinary approaches* (pp. 325-346). Baltimore: University Park.

Light, R. J. (1973). Abused and neglected children in America: A study of alternative policies. *Harvard Educational Review, 43,* 556-598.

Lipowski, Z. J. (1977). Psychosomatic medicine in the seventies: An overview. *American Journal of Psychiatry, 134,* 233-244.

Lipsitt, L. P. (1986). Comment on relations between pediatrics and child development scholarship. *SRCD Newsletter* (Suppl.), pp. 11-13.

Lloyd, J. K., & Wolff, O. H. (1980). Overnutrition and obesity. In F. Falkner (Ed.), *Prevention in childhood of health problems in adult life* (pp. 53-70). Geneva: World Health Organization.

Long, R. T., & Cope, O. (1961). Emotional problems of burned children. *The New England Journal of Medicine, 264,* 1121-1127.

Lovibond, S. H., & Coote, M. A. (1970). Enuresis. In C. G. Costello (Ed.), *Symptoms of psychopathology: A handbook* (pp. 373- 396). New York: Wiley.

Lowe, K., & Lutzker, J. R. (1979). Increasing compliance to a medical regimen with a juvenile diabetic. *Behavior Therapy, 10,* 57-64.

Lubar, J. F., & Bahler, W. W. (1976). Behavioral management of epileptic seizures following EEG biofeedback training of the sensorimotor rhythm. *Biofeedback and Self-Regulation, 1,* 77-104.

Mackay, A. M., & Rothman, K. J. (1982). The incidence and severity of burn injuries following Project Burn Prevention. *American Journal of Public Health, 72,* 248-252.

Madden, N. A., Russo, D. C., & Cataldo, M. F. (1980). Behavioral treatment of pica in children with lead poisoning. *Child Behavior Therapy, 2,* 67-81.

Maddison, B., & Raphael, B. (1971). Social and psychological consequences of chronic disease in childhood. *Medical Journal of Australia, 2,* 2165-2170.

Magrab, P. R., & Calcagno, P. L. (1978). Psychological impact of chronic pediatric conditions. In P. R. Magrab (Ed.), *Psychological management of pediatric problems* (Vol. 1, pp. 3-14). Baltimore: University Park.

Magrab, P. R., & Lehr, E. (1982). Assessment techniques in pediatric psychology. In J. Tuma (Ed.), *Handbook for the practice of pediatric psychology* (pp. 67-109). New York: Wiley.

Magrab, P. R., & Papadopoulou, Z. L. (1977). The effect of a token economy on dietary compliance for children on meodialysis. *Journal of Applied Behavior Analysis, 10,* 573-578.

Magrab, P. R., Sostek, A. M., & Powell, B. A. (1984). Prevention in the perinatal period. In M. C. Roberts & L. Peterson (Eds.), *Prevention of problems in childhood: Psychological research and applications* (pp. 43-73). New York: Wiley.

Maher, B. (1983). The education of health psychologists: Quality counts—Numbers are dangerous. *Health Psychology, 2,* 37-47.

Mallick, M. J. (1983). Health hazards of obesity and weight control in children: A review of the literature. *American Journal of Public Health, 73,* 78-82.

Mallick, S. K., & McCandless, B. R. (1966). A study of catharsis of aggression. *Journal of Personality and Social Psychology, 4,* 591-596.

Manella, K. J., & Varni, J. W. (1981). Behavior therapy in a gait-training program for a child with myelomeningocele. *Physical Therapy, 61,* 1284-1287.

Martens, L. W., Frazier, P. J., Hirt, K. J., Meskin, L. H., & Proshek, J. (1973). Developing brushing performance in second graders through behavior modification. *Health Services Reports, 88,* 818-823.

Martin, H. P., & Rodenhoffer, M. A. (1976). The psychological impact of abuse on children. *Journal of Pediatric Psychology, 1,* 12-15.

Mason, E. A. (1978). Hospital and family cooperating to reduce psychological trauma. *Community Mental Health Journal, 14,* 153-159.

Massey, E. W., & Riley, T. L. (1980). Pseudoseizures: Recognition and treatment. *Psychosomatics, 21,* 987-997.

Matarazzo, J. D. (1980). Behavioral health and behavioral medicine: Frontiers for a new health psychology. *American Psychologist, 35,* 807-817.

Matarazzo, J. D., & Daniel, R. S. (1957). Psychologists in medical schools. *Neuropsychiatry, 4,* 93-107.

Matheny, A. (1988). Prevention of accidental injury. In D. K. Routh (Ed.), *Handbook of pediatric psychology* (pp. 108-134). New York: Guilford.

Mattson, A. (1972). Long-term physical illness in childhood: A challenge to psychosocial adaptation. *Pediatrics, 50,* 801-805.

McCain, E. C. (1982). Parent created tape recordings for hospitalized children. *Journal of the Association for the Care of Children's Health, 10,* 104-105.

McNabb, W. L., Wilson-Pessano, S. R., & Jacobs, A. M. (1986). Critical self-management competencies for children with asthma. *Journal of Pediatric Psychology, 11,* 103-117.

Meadow, R. (1977). Munchausen Syndrome by Proxy: The hinterland of child abuse. *Lancet, 2,* 343-345.

Meichenbaum, D. H., & Goodman, J. (1971). Training impulsive children to talk to themselves: A means of developing self-control. *Journal of Abnormal Psychology, 77,* 115-126.

Melamed, B. G. (1982). Reduction of medical fears: An information processing analysis. In J. Boulougouris (Ed.), *Learning theory approaches to psychiatry* (pp. 205-218). New York: Wiley.

Melamed, B. G., & Bush, J. P. (1985). Family factors in children with acute illness. In D. Turk & R. Kearns (Eds.), *Health, illness, and families: A life-span perspective* (pp. 183-219). New York: Wiley.

Melamed, B. G., Dearborn, M., & Hermecz, D. A. (1983). Necessary considerations for surgery preparation: Age and previous experience. *Psychosomatic Medicine, 45,* 517-525.

Melamed, B. G., Robbins, R. L., & Fernandez, J. (1982). Factors to be considered in psychological preparation for surgery. In D. Routh & M. Wolraich (Eds.), *Advances in developmental and behavioral pediatrics* (pp. 51-72). New York: JAI.

Melamed, B. G., & Siegel, L. J. (1975). Reduction of anxiety in children facing hospitalization and surgery by use of filmed modeling. *Journal of Consulting and Clinical Psychology, 43,* 511-521.

Melamed, B. G., & Siegel, L. J. (1980). *Behavioral medicine: Practical application in health care.* New York: Springer.

Meng, A., & Zastowny, T. (1982). Preparation for hospitalization: A stress inoculation training program for parents and children. *Maternal-Child Nursing Journal, 11,* 87-94.

Mensh, I. N. (1962). Psychology and other professions. In W. B. Webb (Ed.), *The profession of psychology* (pp. 232-252). New York: Holt, Rinehart, & Winston.

Mercer, J. R. (1973). *Labeling the mentally retarded.* Berkeley: University of California Press.

Mercer, J. R. (1979). *Technical manual: SOMPA: System of multicultural pluralistic assessment.* New York: Psychological Corporation.

Mesibov, G. B. (1984). Evolution of pediatric psychology: Historical roots to future trends. *Journal of Pediatric Psychology, 9,* 3-11.

Mesibov, G. B., & Johnson, M. R. (1982). Intervention techniques in pediatric psychology. In J. M. Tuma (Ed.), *Handbook for the practice of pediatric psychology* (pp. 110-164). New York: Wiley.

Miles, M. S., & Carter, M. C. (1982). Sources of parental stress in pediatric intensive care units. *Children's Health Care, 11,* 65-69.

Miller, A. J., & Kratochwill, T. R. (1979). Reduction of frequent stomachache complaints by time out. *Behavior Therapy, 10,* 211-218.

Minuchin, S. (1974). *Families and family therapy.* Cambridge, MA: Harvard University Press.

Minuchin, S., Rossman, B. L., & Baker, L. (1978). *Psychosomatic families.* Cambridge, MA: Harvard University Press.

Money, J. (1977). The syndrome of abuse dwarfism (psychosocial dwarfism or reversible hyposomatotropism): Behavioral data and case report. *American Journal of Disabled Children, 131,* 508-513.

Murphy, L. B. (1974). Coping, vulnerability, and resilience in childhood. In G. V. Coelho, D. A. Haburg, & J. E. Adams (Eds.), *Coping and adaptation* (pp. 69-100). New York: Basic.

Murphy, L. B., & Moriarty, A. E. (1976). *Vulnerability, coping, and growth: From infancy to adolescence*. New Haven, CT: Yale University Press.

Natapoff, J. (1978). Children's views of health: A developmental study. *American Journal of Public Health, 68*, 995-1000.

Nathan, R. G., Lubin, B., Matarazzo, J. D., & Persely, G. W. (1979). Psychologists in schools of medicine: 1955, 1964, and 1977. *American Psychologist, 34*, 622-627.

Naylor, K. A., & Mattson, A. (1973). "For the sake of the children": Trials and tribulations of child psychiatry-liaison service. *Psychiatry in Medicine, 4*, 389-403.

Newberger, E. H., & Bourne, R. (1978). The medicalization and legalization of child abuse. *American Journal of Orthopsychiatry, 48*, 593-607.

Nocella, J., & Kaplan, R. M. (1982). Training children to cope with dental treatment. *Journal of Pediatric Psychology, 7*, 175-178.

Ollendick, T. H. (1979). Fear reduction techniques with children. In M. Hersen, R. M. Eisler, & P. M. Miller (Eds.), *Progress in behavior modification* (Vol. 8, pp. 127-168). New York: Academic.

O'Meara, K., McAuliffe, M. J., Motherway, D., & Dunleavy, M. J. (1983). Preadmission programs: Development, implementation, and evaluation. *Journal of the Association for the Care of Children's Health, 11*, 137-141.

Oster, J. (1972). Recurrent abdominal pain, headache and limb pains in children and adolescents. *Pediatrics, 50*, 429-436.

Ottinger, D. K., & Roberts, M. C. (1980). A university-based predoctoral practicum in pediatric psychology. *Professional Psychology, 11*, 707-713.

Outwater, K. M., Lipnick, R. N., Luban, N. C., Ravenscroft, K., & Ruley, E. J. (1981). Factitious hematuria: Diagnosis by minor blood group typing. *Journal of Pediatrics, 98*, 95-97.

Parke, R. D., & O'Leary, S. (1976). Family interaction in the newborn period: Some findings, some observations, and some unresolved issues. In M. K. Riegel & J. Meacham (Eds.), *The developing individual in a changing world: Vol 2. Social and environmental issues* (pp. 653-663). The Hague: Mouton.

Parmelee, A. H. (1986). Children's illnesses: Their beneficial effects on behavioral development. *Child Development, 57*, 1-10.

Patterson, G. R., & Gullion, M. E. (1968). *Living with children: New methods for parents and teachers*. Champaign, IL: Research Press.

Paul, G. L. (1967). Strategy of outcome research in psychotherapy. *Journal of Consulting Psychology, 31*, 109-118.

Paulson, M. J., & Chaleff, A. (1973). Parent surrogate roles: A dynamic concept in understanding and treating abusive parents. *Journal of Clinical Child Psychology, 2*, 38-40.

Perry, S., & Heidrich, G. (1982). Management of pain during debridement: A survey of U.S. burn units. *Pain, 13,* 267-280.

Peterson, E. (1972). The impact of adolescent illness on parental relationships. *Journal of Health and Social Behavior, 13,* 429-437.

Peterson, L. (1984a). The "Safe at Home" game: Training comprehensive prevention skills in latchkey children. *Behavior Modification, 8,* 474-494.

Peterson, L. (1984b). Teaching home safety and survival skills to latch-key children: A comparison of two manuals and methods. *Journal of Applied Behavior Analysis, 17,* 279-294.

Peterson, L. (in press). Coping by children undergoing stressful medical procedures: Some conceptual, methodological, and therapeutic issues. *Journal of Consulting and Clinical Psychology.*

Peterson, L., & Brownlee-Duffeck, M. (1984). Prevention of anxiety and pain due to medical and dental procedures. In M. C. Roberts & L. Peterson (Eds.), *Prevention of problems in childhood: Psychological research and applications* (pp. 266-308). New York: Wiley.

Peterson, L., & Burbach, D. J. (in press). Historical trends in treating childhood psychopathology. In J. L. Matson (Ed.), *Handbook for treatment approaches in childhood psychopathology.* New York: Plenum.

Peterson, L., Farmer, J., & Mori, L. (1987). Process analysis of injury situations: A complement to epidemiological methods. *Journal of Social Issues, 43,* 33-44.

Peterson, L., & Mori, L. (1985). Prevention of child injury: An overview of targets, methods, and tactics for psychology. *Journal of Consulting and Clinical Psychology, 53,* 586-595.

Peterson, L., & Mori, L. (1987). Multimodal behavioral assessment of children in stressful medical settings. In R. Prinz (Ed.), *Advances in behavioral assessment of children and families* (pp. 35-36). Greenwich, CT: JAI.

Peterson, L., & Mori, L. (1988). Preparation for hospitalization. In D. K. Routh (Ed.), *Handbook of pediatric psychology* (pp. 460-491). New York: Guilford.

Peterson, L., Mori, L., & Carter, P. (1985). The role of the family in children's responses to stressful medical procedures. *Journal of Clinical Child Psychology, 14,* 98-104.

Peterson, L., Mori, L., Selby, V., & Rosen, B. (1988). Community interventions in children's injury prevention: Differing costs and differing benefits. *Journal of Community Psychology, 16,* 188-204.

Peterson, L., & Ridley-Johnson, R. (1983). Prevention of disorders in children. In C. Walker & M. C. Roberts (Eds.), *Handbook of clinical child psychology* (pp. 1174-1197). New York: Wiley.

Peterson, L., Ridley-Johnson, R., Tracy, K., & Mullins, L. L. (1984). Developing cost-effective presurgical preparation: A comparative analysis. *Journal of Pediatric Psychology, 9,* 274-296.

Peterson, L., Schultheis, K., Ridley-Johnson, R., Miller, D. V., & Tracy, K. C. (1984). Comparison of three modeling procedures on the presurgical and postsurgical reactions of children. *Behavior Therapy, 15,* 197-203.

Peterson, L., & Shigetomi, C. (1981). The use of coping techniques to minimize anxiety in hospitalized children. *Behavior Therapy, 12,* 1-14.

Peterson, L., & Shigetomi, C. (1982). One-year follow-up of elective surgery child patients receiving preoperative preparation. *Journal of Pediatric Psychology, 7,* 43-48.

Peterson, L., & Toler, S. M. (1986). An information seeking disposition in child surgery patients: Some preliminary evidence. *Health Psychology, 5,* 343-358.

Petrie, P. A., Kratochwill, T. R., Bergan, J. R., & Nicholson, G. I. (1981). Teaching parents to teach their children: Applications in the pediatric setting. *Journal of Pediatric Psychology, 6,* 275-292.

Petrillo, M., & Sanger, S. (1972). *Emotional care of hospitalized children.* Philadelphia: Lippincott.

Piaget, J. (1950). *The psychology of intelligence.* London: Routledge & Kegan Paul.

Piaget, J. (1970). Piaget's theory. In P. E. Mussen (Ed.), *Carmichael's manual of child psychology* (Vol. 1, 3rd ed., pp. 703-732). New York: Wiley.

Pidgeon, V. (1981). Function of preschool children's questions in coping with hospitalization. *Research in Nursing and Health, 4,* 229-235.

Pinkerton, S. S., Hughes, H., & Wenrich, W. W. (1982). *Behavioral medicine: Clinical applications.* New York: Wiley.

Pinto, R. P., & Hollandsworth, J. G., Jr. (in press). Evaluation of psychological preparation of pediatric surgery: The influence of parents on preparation and the cost vs. benefits of providing preparation services. *Health Psychology.*

Pless, I. B. (1978). Accident prevention and health education: Back to the drawing board? *Pediatrics, 62,* 431-435.

Pless, I. B., & Pinkerton, P. (1975). *Chronic childhood disorder: Promoting patterns of adjustment.* Chicago: Year Book Medical.

Poche, C., Brouwer, R., & Swearingen, M. (1981). Teaching self-protection to young children. *Journal of Applied Behavior Analysis, 14,* 169-176.

Poster, E. C. (1983). Stress immunization: Techniques to help children cope with hospitalization. *Maternal-Child Nursing Journal, 12,* 119-134.

Poznanski, E. O. (1979). The hospitalized child. In J. D. Noshpitz (Ed.), *Basic handbook of child psychiatry* (Vol. 3, pp. 567-577). New York: Basic.

Primack, W. A., & Greifer, I. (1977). Summer camp hemodialysis for children with chronic renal failure. *Pediatrics, 60,* 46-50.

Prugh, D. G., & Jordan, K. (1975). Physical illness or injury: The hospital as a source of emotional disturbances in child and family. In I. N. Berlin (Ed.), *Advocacy for child mental health* (pp. 208-249). New York: Brunner/Mazel.

Prugh, D. G., Staub, E. M., Sands, H. H., Kirschbaum, R. M., & Lenihan, E. A. (1953). A study of the emotional reactions of children and families to hospitalization and illness. *American Journal of Orthopsychiatry, 23,* 70-106.

Ramsden, R., Friedman, B., & Williamson, D. (1983). Treatment of childhood headache reports with contingency management procedures. *Journal of Clinical Child Psychology, 12,* 202-206.

Rapoff, M. A., & Christophersen, E. R. (1982). Improving compliance in pediatric practice. *Pediatric Clinics of North America, 29,* 339-357.

Rapoff, M. A., Christophersen, E. R., & Rapoff, K. E. (1982). The management of common childhood bedtime problems by pediatric nurse practitioners. *Journal of Pediatric Psychology, 7,* 179-196.

Rapoff, M. A., Lindsley, C. B., & Christophersen, E. R. (in press). Improving compliance with medical regimens: A case study with juvenile rheumatoid arthritis. *Archives of Physical Medicine and Rehabilitation.*

Rathus, S. A. (1988). *Understanding child development.* New York: Holt, Rinehart, & Winston.

Redd, W. H. (1980). Stimulus control and extinction of psychosomatic symptoms in cancer patients in protective isolation. *Journal of Consulting and Clinical Psychology, 48,* 448-455.

Reidy, T. J. (1977). The aggressive characteristics of abused and neglected children. *Journal of Clinical Psychology, 3,* 1140-1145.

Reschly, D. J. (1981). Psychological testing in educational classification and placement. *American Psychologist, 36,* 1159-1166.

Reynold, E. H. (1978). Drug treatment of epilepsy. *Lancet, 2,* 721-725.

Rivara, F. P., & Barber, M. (1985). Demographic analysis of childhood pedestrian injuries. *Pediatrics, 75,* 375-387.

Roberts, M. C. (1979, August). *Clinical child psychology programs: Where and what are they?* Paper presented at the meeting of the American Psychological Association, New York.

Roberts, M. C. (1982). Clinical child psychology programs: Where and what are they? *Journal of Clinical Child Psychology, 11,* 13-21.

Roberts, M. C. (1986). *Pediatric psychology: Psychological interventions and strategies for pediatric problems.* New York: Pergamon.

Roberts, M. C., Beidleman, W. B., & Wurtele, S. (1981). Children's perceptions of medical and psychological disorders in their peers. *Journal of Clinical Child Psychology, 10,* 76-78.

Roberts, M. C., Elkins, P. D., & Royal, G. D. (1984). Psychological applications to the prevention of accidents and illness. In M. C. Roberts & L. Peterson (Eds.), *Prevention of problems in childhood: Psychological research and applications* (pp. 173-199). New York: Wiley.

Roberts, M. C., & Funurik, D. (1986). Rewarding elementary school children for their use of safety belts. *Health Psychology, 6,* 185-196.

Roberts, M. C., & Horner, M. M. (1979). A comprehensive intervention for failure-to-thrive. *Journal of Clinical Child Psychology, 8,* 10-14.

Roberts, M. C., Ottinger, D. R., & Hannemann, R. E. (1977). *On treating childhood encopresis.* Unpublished manuscript, Purdue University, West Layfayette, IN.

Roberts, M. C., & Peterson, L. (1984a). Prevention models: Theoretical and practical implications. In M. C. Roberts & L. Peterson (Eds.), *Prevention of problems in childhood: Psychological research and applications* (pp. 1-39). New York: Wiley.

Roberts, M. C., & Peterson, L. (1984b). *Prevention of problems in childhood: Psychological research and applications.* New York: Wiley.

Roberts, M. C., Quevillon, R. P., & Wright, L. (1979). Pediatric psychology: A developmental report and survey of the literature. *Child and Youth Services, 2,* 1-9.

Roberts, M. C., & Wright, L. (1982). Rule of the pediatric psychologist as consultant to pediatricians. In J. Tuma (Ed.), *Handbook for the practice of pediatric psychology* (pp. 251-289). New York: Wiley.

Roberts, M. C., Wurtele, S. K., Boone, R. R., Ginther, C., & Elkins, P. D. (1981). Reduction of medical fears by use of modeling: A preventive application in a general population of children. *Journal of Pediatric Psychology, 6,* 293-300.

Robertson, J. (1958). *Young children in hospitals.* New York: Random House.

Robertson, L. S. (1983). *Injuries: Causes, control strategies, and public policy.* Lexington, MA: Lexington.

Rosen, C. L., Frost, J. D., Bricker, T., Tarnow, J. D., Gillette, P. C., & Dunlavy, S. (1983). Two siblings with recurrent cardiorespiratory arrest: Munchausen Syndrome by Proxy or child abuse? *Pediatrics, 71,* 715-720.

Rosenbaum, M. (1980). A schedule for assessing self-control behaviors: Preliminary findings. *Behavior Therapy, 11,* 109- 121.

Rosenberg, M. S., & Reppucci, N. D. (1985). Primary prevention of child abuse. *Journal of Consulting and Clinical Psychology, 53,* 576-585.

Rosenstock, I. M. (1974). Historical origins of the Health Belief Model. *Health Education Monographs, 2,* 328-335.

Roskies, E., Mongeon, M., & Gagnon-Lefebre, B. (1978). Increasing maternal participation in the hospitalization of young children. *Medical Care, 16,* 765-777.

Rothstein, P. (1980). Psychological stress in families of children in a pediatric intensive care unit. *Pediatric Clinics of North America, 27,* 611-620.

Routh, D. K. (1969). Graduate training in pediatric psychology: The Iowa program. *Pediatric Psychology, 1,* 4-5.

Routh, D. K. (1970). Psychological training in medical school departments of pediatrics: A survey. *Professional Psychology, 1,* 469-472.

Routh, D. K. (1972). Graduate training in medical school departments of pediatrics: A second look. *American Psychologist, 27,* 587-589.

Routh, D. K. (1977). Postdoctoral training in pediatric psychology. *Professional Psychology, 8,* 245-250.

Routh, D. K. (1978). Hyperactivity. In P. R. Magrab (Ed.), *Psychological management of pediatric problems* (Vol. 2, pp. 3- 47). Baltimore: University Park.

Routh, D. K. (1982). Pediatric psychology as an area of scientific research. In J. M. Tuma (Ed.), *Handbook for the practice of pediatric psychology* (pp. 290-320). New York: Wiley.

Routh, D. K. (1988). Introduction. In D. K. Routh (Ed.), *Handbook of pediatric psychology* (pp. 1-5). New York: Guilford.

Routh, D. K., & Ernst, A. R. (1984). Somatization disorder in relatives of children and adolescents with functional abdominal pain. *Journal of Pediatric Psychology, 9,* 427-437.

Routh, D. K., Ernst, A. R., & Harper, D. C. (1988). Recurrent abdominal pain in children with somatization disorder. In D. K. Routh (Ed.), *Handbook of pediatric psychology* (pp. 673-771), New York: Guilford.

Russo, D. C., & Varni, J. W. (1982). *Behavioral prediatrics: Research and practice.* New York: Plenum.

Salk, L. (1970). Psychologist in a pediatric setting. *Professional Psychology, 1,* 395-396.

Salk, L. (1974). Psychologist and pediatrician: A mental health team in the prevention and early diagnosis of mental disorders. In G. I. Williams & S. Gordon (Eds.), *Clinical child psychology: Current practices and future perspectives* (pp. 110-115). New York: Behavioral Publications.

Salk, L. (1978). *What every child would like parents to know about divorce.* New York: Harper & Row.

Sanders, N. R., Rebgetz, M., Morrison, M., Bor, W., Gordon, A., Dadds, M., & Shepherd, R. (in press). Cognitive behavioral treatment of recurrent nonspecific abdominal pain in children: An analysis of generalization maintenance and side effects. *Journal of Consulting and Clinical Psychology.*

Sank, L. I., & Biglan, A. (1974). Operant treatment of a case of recurrent abdominal pain in a 10-year-old boy. *Behavior Therapy, 5,* 677-681.

Saunders, A. M., & Lamb, W. (1977). A group experience with parents of hemophiliacs: A viable alternative to group therapy. *Journal of Clinical Child Psychology, 6,* 79-82.

Scarr, S. (1981). Testing for children: Assessment and the many determinants of intellectual competence. *American Psychologist, 36,* 1159-1166.

Schaffer, A. J. (1967). Advantages of mother living in with her hospitalized child. In J. A. Haller, Jr., J. L. Talbert, & R. H. Dombro (Eds.), *The hospitalized child and his family* (pp. 33-41). Baltimore: Johns Hopkins University Press.

Schoenberger, J. A. (1982). Why cardiovascular health education in the schools: From a medical perspective. *Health Education, 35,* 15-16.

Schowalter, J. E. (1979). Hospital consultation as therapy. In J. D. Noshpitz (Ed.), *Basic handbook of child psychiatry* (Vol. 3, pp. 365-375). New York: Basic.

Schrader, E. S. (1979). Preparation play helps children in hospitals. *AORN Journal, 30,* 336-341.

Schroeder, C. S. (1979). Psychologists in a private pediatric practice. *Journal of Pediatric Psychology, 4,* 5-18.

Schroeder, C. S., Goolsby, E., & Stangler, S. (1975). Preventive services in a private pediatric practice. *Journal of Clinical Child Psychology, 4,* 32-33.

Sergis-Deavenport, E., & Varni, J. W. (1982). Behavioral techniques in teaching hemophilia factor replacement procedures to families. *Pediatric Nursing, 8,* 416-419.

Sergis-Deavenport, E., & Varni, J. W. (1983). Behavioral assessment and management of adherence to factor replacement therapy in hemophilia. *Journal of Pediatric Psychology, 8,* 367-377.

Shaw, E. G., & Routh, D. K. (1982). Effect of mother presence on children's reaction to adverse procedures. *Journal of Pediatric Psychology, 7,* 33-42.

Sheridan, M. S. (1975). Talk time for hospitalized children. *Social Work, 20,* 40-44.

Shipley, R. H., Butt, J. H., & Horwitz, E. (1979). Preparation to reexperience a stressful medical examination: Effect of repetitious videotape exposure and coping style. *Journal of Consulting and Clinical Psychology, 47,* 485-492.

Shipley, R. H., Butt, J. H., Horwitz, B., & Farbry, J. E. (1978). Preparation for a stressful medical procedure: Effect of amount of stimulus preexposure and coping style. *Journal of Consulting and Clinical Psychology, 46,* 499-507.

Siegel, L. J. (1981, April). *Naturalistic study of coping strategies in children facing medical procedures.* Paper presented at the meeting of the Southeastern Psychological Association, Atlanta.

Siegel, L. J., & Peterson, L. (1980). Stress reduction in young dental patients through coping skills and sensory information. *Journal of Consulting and Clinical Psychology, 48,* 785-787.

Siegel, L. J., & Peterson, L. (1981). Maintenance effects of coping skills and sensory information on young children's reponse to repeated dental procedures. *Behavior Therapy, 12,* 530-535.

Siegel, S. E., Dwyer, J., Konig, P., Berman, B., Bierman, W., & Kass, I. (1982). *Pharmacologic management of the problem asthmatic* (Schering Doctor-to-Doctor Series). Captiva Island, FL: Schering Corporation.

Silberstein, R. P., & Galton, L. (1982). *Helping your child grow slim*. New York: Simon & Schuster.

Simeonsson, R. J., Buckley, L., & Monson, L. (1979). Conceptions of illness causality in hospitalized children. *Journal of Pediatric Psychology, 4,* 77-84.

Sipowicz, R. R., & Vernon, D. T. A. (1965). Psychological response of children to hospitalization. *American Journal of Diseases of Children, 109,* 228-231.

Skipper, J. K., & Leonard, R. C. (1968). Children, stress, and hospitalization: A field experiment. *Journal of Health and Social Behavior, 9,* 275-287.

Skipper, J. K., Leonard, R. C., & Rhymes, J. (1968). Child hospitalization and social interaction: An experimental study of mothers' feelings of stress, adaptation and satisfaction. *Medical Care, 6,* 496-506.

Skyler, J. S., & Cahill, G. F., Jr. (1981). Diabetes mellitus: Progress and directions. In J. S. Skyler & G. F. Cahill, Jr. (Eds.), *Diabetes mellitus* (pp. ix-xii). New York: Yorke Medical.

Smetana, J. G., Kelly, M., & Twentyman, C. T. (1984). Abused, neglected, and nonmaltreated children's conceptions of moral and social-conventional transgressions. *Child Development, 55,* 277-287.

Smuts, A. (1986). Introduction. *SRCD Newsletter* (Suppl.), p. 7.

Sostek, A. M., Scanlon, J. W., & Abramson, D. C. (1982). Postpartum contact and maternal confidence and anxiety: A confirmation of short-term effects. *Infant Behavior and Development, 5,* 323-329.

Sourkes, B. M. (1977). Facilitating family coping with childhood cancer. *Journal of Pediatric Psychology, 2,* 65-67.

Spiegel, C. N., & Lindaman, F. C. (1977). Children can't fly: A program to prevent childhood morbidity and mortality from window falls. *American Journal of Public Health, 67,* 1143-1147.

Spinetta, J. J. (1974). The dying child's awareness of death: A review. *Psychological Bulletin, 81,* 256-260.

Spinetta, J. J. (1977). Adjustment in children with cancer. *Journal of Pediatric Psychology, 2,* 49-51.

Spinetta, J. J., Elliott, E. S., Hennessey, J. S., Knapp, V. S., Sheposh, J. P., Sparta, S. N., & Sprigle, R. P. (1982). In J. Tuma (Ed.), *Handbook for the practice of pediatric psychology* (pp. 165-227). New York: Wiley.

SRCD Newsletter. (1986, Suppl.). Chicago, IL: Society for Research in Child Development.

Stabler, B. (1979). Emerging models of psychologist-pediatrician liaison. *Journal of Pediatric Psychology, 4,* 307-313.

Stabler, B. (1988). Pediatric consultation-liaison. In D. K. Routh (Ed.), *Handbook of pediatric psychology* (pp. 538-566). New York: Guilford.

Stabler, B., Fernald, G. W., Johnson, M. R., Johnson, M. P., & Ryan, J. J. (1981). *Facilitating positive prosocial adaptation in children with cystic fibrosis by* increasing family communication and problem solving skills (Research Report). Chapel Hill, NC: University of North Carolina Cystic Fibrosis Foundation. (ERIC Document Reproduction Service No. ED 207 708)

Stabler, B., & Murray, J. P. (1973). Pediatrician's perceptions of pediatric psychology. *Clinical Psychologist, 27*(1), 12-15.

Stabler, B., & Whitt, J. K. (1980). Pediatric psychology: Perspectives and training implications. *Journal of Pediatric Psychology, 5,* 245-251.

Starfield, B. (1977). Health needs of children. In *Children's medical care needs and treatments. Report of the Harvard Health Project* (Vol. 2, pp. 23-40). Cambridge, MA: Ballinger.

Stein, R., & Jessop, D. (1982). A noncategorical approach to chronic childhood illness. *Public Health Reports, 97,* 354-362.

Steinhauer, P., Mushin, D., & Rae-Grant, Q. (1974). Psychological aspects of chronic illness. *Pediatric Clinics of North America, 21,* 825-840.

Steinhausen, H. C. (1976). Hemophilia: A psychological study in chronic disease in juveniles. *Journal of Psychosomatic Research, 20,* 461-467.

Stolz, S. B. (1984). Preventive models: Implications for a technology of practice. In M. C. Roberts & L. Peterson (Eds.), *Prevention of problems in childhood: Psychological research and applications* (pp. 391-413). New York: Wiley.

Stone, R. T., & Barbero, G. J. (1970). Recurrent abdominal pain in childhood. *Pediatrics, 45,* 732.

Strowcynski, H., Stachewitsch, A., Morgen-Stern, G., & Shaw, E. (1973). Delivery of care to hemophilic children: Home care versus hospitalization. *Pediatrics, 51,* 986-991.

Stuart, R., & Davis, B. (1972). *Slim chance in a fat world: Behavioral control of obesity.* Champaign, IL: Research Press.

Swain, J. J., Allard, G. B., & Holborn, S. W. (1982). The Good Toothbrushing Game: A school-based dental hygiene program for increasing the toothbrushing effectiveness of children. *Journal of Applied Behavior Analysis, 15,* 171-176.

Tarnowski, K. J., Kelly, P. A., & Mendlowitz, D. K. (1987). Acceptability of behavioral pediatric interventions. *Journal of Consulting and Clinical Psychology, 55,* 435-436.

Task Force on Training for Division of Child, Youth, and Family Services of the American Psychological Association. (1983). *Recommended minimal training criteria for psychologists working with children, youth, and families.* Washington, DC: American Psychological Association, Division 37.

Task Group on Life Cycle Health Psychology. (1983). *Health Psychology, 2* (Suppl.), 107-109.

Tefft, B. M., & Simeonsson, R. J. (1979). Psychology and the creation of health care settings. *Professional Psychology, 10,* 558-570.

Tertinger, D. A., Greene, B. F., & Lutzker, J. R. (1984). Home safety: Development and validation of one component of an ecobehavioral treatment program for abused and neglected children. *Journal of Applied Behavior Analysis, 17,* 159-174.

Thomas, L. (1980). Patient groups for children who have cancer. In J. L. Schulman & M. J. Kupst (Eds.), *The child with cancer* (pp. 7-15). Springfield, IL: Charles C. Thomas.

Thompson, E. L. (1978). Smoking education programs, 1960-1976. *American Journal of Public Health, 68,* 250-257.

Trause, M. A. (1981). Extra postpartum contact: An assessment of the intervention and its effects. In V. L. Smeriglio (Ed.), *Newborns and parents: Parent-infant contact and newborn sensory stimulation* (pp. 65-74). Hillsdale, NJ: Erlbaum.

Travis, G. (1976). *Chronic illness in children.* Stanford, CA: Stanford University Press.

Tuma, J. M. (1975). Pediatric psychology? . . . Do you mean clinical child psychology? *Journal of Clinical Child Psychology, 4,* 9-12.

Tuma, J. M. (1977). Practicum, internship, and postdoctoral training in pediatric psychology: A survey. *Journal of Pediatric Psychology, 2,* 9-12.

Tuma, J. M. (Ed.). (1980). *Directory: Internship programs in clinical child and pediatric psychology (including postdoctoral training programs)* (2nd ed.). Baton Rouge, LA: Society of Pediatric Psychology.

Tuma, J. M. (1982a). Pediatric psychology: Conceptualization and definition. In J. M. Tuma (Ed.), *Handbook for the practice of pediatric psychology* (pp. 1-27). New York: Wiley.

Tuma, J. M. (1982b). Training in pediatric psychology. In J. M. Tuma (Ed.), *Handbook for the practice of pediatric psychology* (pp. 321-346). New York: Wiley.

Tuma, J. M. (1987). *Directory of internship programs in clinical child and pediatric psychology.* Baton Rouge, LA: Author.

Tuma, J. M., & Grabert, J. (1983). Internship and postdoctoral training in pediatric and clinical child psychology: A survey. *Journal of Pediatric Psychology, 8,* 245-260.

United States Department of Health, Education, and Welfare. (1978). *Health in the United States* (DHEW Publication No. PHS 75-1232). Washington, DC: United States Government Printing Office.

United States Public Health Service. (1979a). *Basic data on dental examination findings of persons 1-74 years, United States, 1971-74* (DHEW, PHS, NCHS

Publication No. PHS 79-1662). Washington, DC: United States Government Printing Office.

United States Public Health Service. (1979b). *Smoking and health: A report of the Surgeon General* (DHEW, PHS Publication No. PHS 79-50066). Washington, DC: United States Government Printing Office.

Uzgiris, I. C., & Hunt, J. M. (1975). *Assessment in infancy.* Urbana: University of Illinois Press.

VandenBos, G. R., Stapp, J., & Kilburg, R. R. (1981). Health service providers in psychology: Results of the 1978 APA human resources survey. *American Psychologist, 36,* 1395-1418.

Varni, J. W. (1981a). Behavioral medicine in hemophilia arthritic pain management: Two case studies. *Archives of Physical Medicine and Rehabilitation, 62,* 183-187.

Varni, J. W. (1981b). Self-regulation techniques in the management of chronic arthritic pain in hemophilia. *Behavior Therapy, 12,* 185-194.

Varni, J. W. (1983). *Clinical behavioral pediatrics: An interdisciplinary biobehavioral approach.* New York: Pergamon.

Varni, J. W., Bessman, C. A., Russo, D. C., & Cataldo, M. F. (1980). Behavioral management of chronic pain in children: Case study. *Archives of Physical Medicine and Rehabilitation, 61,* 375-379.

Varni, J. W., & Gilbert, A. (1982). Self-regulation of chronic arthritic pain and long-term analgesic dependence in a hemophiliac. *Rheumatology and Rehabilitation, 21,* 171-174.

Varni, J. W., Gilbert, A., & Dietrich, S. L. (1981). Behavioral medicine in pain and analgesia management for the hemophilic child with Factor VIII inhibitor. *Pain, 11,* 121-126.

Varni, J. W., & Wallander, J. L. (1984). Adherence to health-related regimens in pediatric chronic disorders. *Clinical Psychology Review, 4,* 585-596.

Venham, L. L. (1973). *The effect of the mother's presence on the child's response to a stressful situation.* Unpublished manuscript, University of Connecticut, Storrs.

Venham, L. L., Bengston, D., & Cipes, M. (1978). Children's response to sequential dental visits. *Journal of Dental Research, 56,* 454-459.

Vernon, D. T. A., & Bailey, W. C. (1974). The use of motion pictures in the psychological preparation of children for induction of anesthesia. *Anesthesiology, 40,* 68-74.

Vernon, D. T. A., Foley, J. M., & Schulman, J. L. (1967). Effect of mother-child separation and birth order on young children's responses to two potentially stressful experiences. *Journal of Personality and Social Psychology, 5,* 162-174.

Voller, R. D., & Strong, W. B. (1981). Pediatric aspects of atherosclerosis. *American Heart Journal, 101,* 815-836.

Wakeman, R. J., & Kaplan, J. Z. (1978). An experimental study of hypnosis in painful burns. *American Journal of Clinical Hypnosis, 21,* 3-12.

Walker, C. E. (1979). Behavioral intervention in a pediatric setting. In J. R. Mac-Namara (Ed.), *Behavioral approaches in medicine: Application and analysis* (pp. 227-266). New York: Plenum.

Walker, C. E., Miller, M. D., & Smith, R. (1985). An introduction to pediatric psychology. In P. Keller & L. Ritt (Eds.), *Innovations in clinical practice: A source book* (Vol. 4, pp. 415-434). Sarasota, FL: Professional Resource Exchange.

Walker, C. E., Milling, L., & Bonner, B. L. (1988). Incontinence disorders: Enuresis and encopresis. In D. K. Routh (Ed.), *Handbook of pediatric psychology* (pp. 363-397). New York: Guilford.

Walton, W. W. (1982). An evaluation of the Poison Prevention Packaging Act. *Pediatrics, 69,* 363-370.

Watkins, J. D., Roberts, D. E., Williams, T. F., Martin, D. A., & Coyle, V. (1967). Observation of medication errors made by diabetic patients in the home. *Diabetes, 16,* 882-885.

Waxman, M., & Stunkard, A. J. (1980). Caloric intake and expenditure of obese boys. *Journal of Pediatrics, 96,* 187-193.

Weinstein, D. J. (1976). Imagery and relaxation with a burn patient. *Behavior Research and Therapy, 14,* 481.

White, B. L., Watts, J. C., Barnett, I. C., Kaban, B. T., Marmor, J. R., & Shapiro, B. B. (1973). *Experience and environment: Major influences on the development of the young child.* Englewood Cliffs, NJ: Prentice-Hall.

White, J. R. (1973). Effects of a counterirritant on perceived pain and hand movement in patients with arthritis. *Physical Therapy, 53,* 956-960.

Whitehead, W. E., Parker, L. H., Masek, B. J., Cataldo, M. F., & Freeman, J. M. (1981). Biofeedback treatment of fecal incontinence in patients with myelomemingocele. *Developmental Medicine and Child Neurology, 23,* 313-322.

Whitt, J. K., & Casey, P. H. (1982). The mother-infant relationship and infant development: The effect of pediatric intervention. *Child Development, 53,* 948-956.

Whitt, J. K., Dykstra, W., & Taylor, C. A. (1979). Children's conceptions of illness and cognitive development: Implications for pediatric practitioners. *Clinical Pediatrics, 18,* 327-339.

Widmayer, S. M., & Field, T. M. (1980). Effects of Brazelton demonstration on early interactions of preterm infants and their teenage mothers. *Infant Behavior and Development, 3,* 79-89.

Williams, D. T., Spiegel, H., & Mostofsky, D. I. (1978). Neurogenic and hysterical seizures in children and adolescents: Differential diagnostic and therapeutic considerations. *American Journal of Psychiatry, 135,* 82-86.

Williams, G. J. (1978). Child abuse. In P. R. Magrab (Ed.), *Psychological management of pediatric problems* (Vol. 1, pp. 253-291). Baltimore: University Park.

Williams, P. (1978a). Children's concepts of illness and internal body parts. *Maternal-Child Nursing Journal, 1,* 115-123.

Williams, P. (1978b). A comparison of Philippine and American children's concepts of body organs and illness in relation to five variables. *International Journal of Nursing Studies, 15,* 193-202.

Williams, T. F., Martin, D. A., Hogan, M. D., Watkins, J. D., & Ellis, E. V. (1967). The clinical picture of diabetic control studied in four settings. *American Journal of Public Health, 57,* 441-451.

Willis, D. J. (1976). Editorial: A preventive model for child abuse. *Journal of Pediatric Psychology, 1,* 98.

Willis, D. J., Elliott, C. H., & Jay, S. M. (1982). Psychological effects of physical illness and its concomitants. In J. Tuma (Ed.), *Handbook for the practice of pediatric psychology* (pp. 28-66). New York: Wiley.

Wilson, A. M. (1982). A familiar face. *Anaesthesia, 37,* 1225.

Wilson, J. F. (1981). Behavioral preparation for surgery: Benefit or harm? *Journal of Behavioral Medicine, 4,* 79-101.

Wolfer, J. A., & Visintainer, M. A. (1975). Pediatric surgery patients' and parents' stress responses and adjustment. *Nursing Research, 24,* 244-255.

Work, H. (1986). Contributions of child development to the practice of pediatrics. *SRCD Newsletter* (Suppl.), pp. 9-11.

Wright, L. (1967). The pediatric psychologist: A role model. *American Psychologist, 22,* 323-325.

Wright, L. (1972). Intellectual sequelae of Rocky Mountain spotted fever. *Journal of Abnormal Psychology, 80,* 315-316.

Wright, L. (1978). Health care psychology: Prospects for the well-being of children. *American Psychologist, 34,* 1001-1006.

Wright, L. (1979). A comprehensive program for mental health and behavioral medicine in a large children's hospital. *Professional Psychology, 10,* 458-466.

Yeaton, W. H., & Bailey, J. S. (1978). Teaching pedestrian safety skills to young children. An analysis and one-year follow-up. *Journal of Applied Behavior Analysis, 11,* 315-329.

Zastowny, T. R., Kirschenbaum, D. S., & Meng, A. L. (1986). Coping skills training for children: Effects on distress before, during, and after hospitalization for surgery. *Health Psychology, 5,* 231-247.

Zeltzer, L., & LeBaron, S. (1982). Hypnosis and nonhypnotic techniques for reduction of pain and anxiety during painful procedures in children and adolescents with cancer. *Journal of Pediatrics, 101,* 1032-1035.

Zlutnick, S., Mayville, W. J., & Moffat, S. (1975). Modification of seizure disorders: The interruption of behavioral chains. *Journal of Applied Behavior Analysis, 8,* 1-12.

Author Index

Subject Index

177

About the Authors

Lizette Peterson received her Ph.D. from the University of Utah. She is currently Professor of Psychology at the University of Missouri-Columbia and Associate Editor of the *Journal of Consulting and Clinical Psychology*. A Fellow of the Developmental and Community Psychology Divisions of the American Psychological Association, she co-authored with Michael C. Roberts the volume *Prevention of Problems in Childhood*, the first text on that subject, and, with Donna M. Gelfand, the book *Child Development and Psychopathology*. In addition, Dr. Peterson has published over 80 articles and book chapters. In 1988, she won the Society for Pediatric Psychology Significant Research Contributions Award.

Cynthia Harbeck received her B.A. from Augustana College in 1985. She received her M.A. in psychology from the University of Missouri-Columbia and is currently working on her Ph.D. there. She has been involved in studies of children's conceptualization of pain, childhood injuries, psychological preparation for surgery, and addictive behaviors.